DIRT SONGS:
A Plains Duet

Twyla M. Hansen

TWYLA M. HANSEN
Nebraska State Poet 2013-18
nebraskastatepoet2@gmail.com

Linda M. Hasselstrom

LINDA M. HASSELSTROM
Windbreak House
info@windbreakhouse.com

DIRT SONGS:
A Plains Duet

POEMS

Twyla M. Hansen
Linda M. Hasselstrom

The Backwaters Press

First Printing: October 2011

Published by: The Backwaters Press
                  Greg Kosmicki, Rich Wyatt, Editors
                  3502 N. 52nd Street
                  Omaha, NE 68104-3506
                  http://www.thebackwaterspress.org
                  thebackwaterspress@gmail.com

ISBN: 978-1-935218-24-1

Acknowledgments: Twyla M. Hansen

Many thanks to the editors of the publications where these poems first appeared:

Ascent: "Procrastination"; *The Flintlock* 50th Anniversary issue: "Egg" and "Bird"; *Kalliope:* "My Granddaughter Sick"; *Midwest Quarterly* special tribute to Ted Kooser issue: "The Cardinal" and special Nebraska issue: "After A Rain"; *Mystic River Review* (online): "Survival"; *Natural Bridge:* "Swiss Cheese" and "Leap of Faith"; *Paddlefish:* "Returning to St. Louis, Lewis and Clark See a Cow" and "Small"; *Plains Song Review:* "Little Bluestem," "Corn," "Acts of Faith" and "Ornamentals"; *Platte Valley Review:* "My Husband's Grandmother Worked for Willa Cather"; "Swallows," "My Granddaughter Sick," "Shadows," "Taking the Young Child," "Early Winter" and "July" were published in the limited edition chapbook *Sanctuary Near Salt Creek* © 2001 Twyla Hansen, Lone Willow Press; *Crazy Woman Creek: Women Rewrite the American West* Eds. Linda Hasselstrom, Gaydell Collier, Nancy Curtis, 2004 Houghton Mifflin: "Greasy Spoon"; "Taking the Young Child," "Early Winter" and "July" were published as limited edition fine press art books, Ed./Artist Brian Curling © 2005 Goldfinch Press; *Red Thread, Gold Thread: the Poet's Voice* Ed. Alan Cohen, Logan, OH 2009: "August 12 in the Nebraska Sand Hills Watching the Perseids Meteor Shower"; *The Untidy Season: Poetry by Nebraska Women* Eds. Heidi Hermanson, Liz Kay, Jennifer Lambert and Sarah Mason, 2012 The Backwaters Press: "Near the Platte."

"Morning Fog" is reprinted from *Prairie Schooner*, by permission of the University of Nebraska Press, © 2003 University of Nebraska Press

Acknowledgments: Linda M. Hasselstrom

My thanks to the editors of the following publications in which some of these poems first appeared in slightly different form:

Dry Crik (online): "Instead of a Death Watch" and "My Uncle Harold Makes Up His Mind"; *High Desert Journal:* "Autochthonous"; *Red Weather* and *South Dakota Review:* "One Afternoon in a Reservation Classroom"; *South Dakota Review:* "1971: Establishing Perpetual Care at the Locust Grove Baptist Cemetery"; *South Dakota Review:* "When a Poet Dies"; *Wyoming Fence Lines*, Ed. David Romtvedt, 2007 Wyoming Humanities Council and Wyoming Arts

Council: "Visiting Writer in Rock Springs, Wyoming"; *A Harvest of Words: Contemporary South Dakota Poetry*, Ed. Patrick Hicks, 2010 Augustana College Center for Western Studies: "My Mother's Cosmos"; *Cowboy Poetry: The Reunion*, 2004 Gibbs Smith: "Priests of the Prairie"; *No Place Like Home* © 2009 Linda Hasselstrom, University of Nevada Press; and at P3 (Painters, Poets & Pavilion) invitational exhibit, Sioux Falls, SD 2009: "Waiting for the Storm"; P3 (Painters, Poets & Pavilion) invitational exhibit, Sioux Falls, SD 2010: "Lost and Found"; *Windbreak House* (online): "I Ain't Blind and This is What I Think I See," and "Studying Pumice"; "Those Thanksgiving Pie-Makers" was first published as poster for an *Empty Bowls* fundraiser event, United Church of Christ, Brookings, SD, 2006; In "Lost in the City Again," the quotation is by McCarthy Coyle from "Weather Reports" in *Northern Lights*

—to the memory
of our friend and mentor
William C. Kloefkorn
1932–2011

One: Twyla M. Hansen

Two: Linda M. Hasselstrom

One:
Twyla M. Hansen

*—to my foremothers
and to my family*

Morning Fog

In early fall I walk over Salt Creek, breathing air out of the north,
air cooler than the ground, fog rising off the water, and

I pass through, taking in all my nose, my throat
will allow, into lungs air that has arrived here from Canada

southward, the jet stream sagging, bringing particles
off the northern Plains, sucking up dust off farmsteads,

off feedlots and hog factories, exhaust of giant equipment
working vast acreages, row crops to feed all those animals,

their waste collected in clay pits, leaking into lakes, streams,
into groundwater, rivers ripe with nitrates, smoke off

ethanol plants, methane over landfills, air off processing plants,
of pesticides and fertilizers, over ranches and casinos, exhaust

over interstate highways and those nameless 24/7 places
at every intersection, over open spaces with shrinking populations,

cities that keep growing, this city and its sprawl and slow choke
of traffic, heated air off roofs and concrete, it's all around us

whether we like it or not, and we're all here now, in early fall walking
over Salt Creek, breathing the collective air, right under our noses.

Corn

Bin collapse traps Iowa family
in flood of corn.—news article

Imagine a tidal wave of corn
sweeping across the Plains.

Shaking the ground,
knocking houses off foundations,
trapping families inside.

Waiting for hours to be rescued,
buried alive by kernels.

What with corn in the food,
corn in the animal feed,
corn on your tax bill.

Singular crop to erode soil,
drive prices, consume margins.

Sucking up groundwater,
polluting the same,
lining pockets of agribiz.

One field after another—fools' gold—
planted sea to shining sea.

Half a million bushels popped
the rivets, collapsed the roof,
crushed the house, kept on rolling.

A bin 90 feet high, 100 feet around.
Buried alive four hours; oxygen supplied.

No warning, just a sudden machine-gun
noise, just a man-made natural disaster
next to someone's home, waiting.

Afterward, they shake their heads, can't
imagine how this could ever happen.

Acts of Faith

It's an act of faith, hanging wet clothes out on the line
on a clouded morning, to believe that today the music we know
as wind will spin down from heaven with sufficient solar-fire

to wither away all dampness, that my passé ritual each week
in some tiny way might appease the god of all atmosphere
who rides in a balloon over our heated planet, rising, rising.

***

I pierce the soil, plant a seed, mulch with a multitude of leaves,
rotted. When was the last time you meditated on all fours, felt
this pulse of thin crust in your palm, breathed the living miracle
beneath the soles of us all? We trust the farmer to conserve, to produce,

at the same time cripple by policy. No one confesses, yet bubbles
from the farm belt float down the Mississippi into the Gulf, create
a dead zone the size of Jersey. On the altar of growth, in the name
of the almighty dollar, we're treating our soil like dirt.

***

It's all connected: the moon, the protective parasol of overhead air,
water just below this upside-down saucer of earth. Groundwater,
in an extended aquifer sonata on its slow-moving conveyor belt
toward stream and river. That so much depends on a wheelbarrow
left out to rust in the rain, that we must have faith, must truly believe,

must not squander from those who follow. Water: the next oil?
Never in a millennia did we consume so fast and far, this god-nectar,
the stuff that has fueled fortune and famine. Can we afford to fail,
not to worship? Water wild and pure, in your blood and mine,
our bodies clothed from soil, filled with breath, lucky to be alive.

Ornamentals

My friend writes that he doesn't understand ornamentals,
why some fool would breed a peach until it bursts each spring
into an aromatic profusion of bloom, but not produce a single fruit.

Fred, where should I begin? Capitalism? The free market?
Biotech, behind its secretive door wearing its white lab coat,
gone mad? Funny world, isn't it, where everything has its price.

Food, for example, processed to death, animals in confinement
factories, soil beneath mega-monocultures disappearing, silent.
Even nostalgia, in futures trading, quaintly bought and sold.

I grew up rural, too, boomer on the cusp of farming's downfall,
from no-nonsense parent stock who had no idea of the coup
about to take place, the American small-farmer diaspora,

that within a generation, stewardship would unravel like so many
strands of DNA, that cities would swell with wage-earners,
folks whose children and their children have no idea where

nourishment comes from, how food is raised, looking out suburban
windows toward this seedless ash, that fruitless crab, over non-forage
lawn grass now glorified into a seamless carpet of green.

Little Bluestem

Schizachyrium scoparium, Nebraska's State Grass

Neither little or blue, its fine stems know
the ways of travelers—
animal, human, otherwise.
Thrived for millennia throughout the Plains,

resisting drought, wind, hail, cold, heat,
fire by man or heaven.
Silent against all but the sturdiest plow,
the heaviest grazer.

Yielding its excellent forage.
Sod extensive, forming
the richest farming soils on earth.
Irony abounds in the all-outdoors.

A seasonal garden palette: pale gray—
green to darker, silvery flower-stalks in fall,
a blaze of red-orange in winter.
Plentiful seed for the birds.

Designated by Legislature, designed
by Nature—*are you listening?*—
roots sniffing down to bones
of an ancient sea.

Survival

Where soil is dry,
weather inhospitable,
no one watching,
red cedars thrive.

> Invading
the unplowed field, grassland, true
to their youth-producing roots—*juniperus*—
their berry-like seeds' dormancy removed,
all inhibitors, by the scouring action
of bird-gut.

> Prolific as weeds, the familiar
breeding contempt. Sprouting anywhere,
the strange and twisted life of flora.
An evergreen the ecologist loves to hate,
gleeful at the ignition, explosion, when burning
to manage a prairie.

> Yet their maze of shapes,
their common purple shadow draws
the inland eye. Driving the Plains in winter,
I can't help but notice them,
their wind-battered limbs, clinging
to some grand obtuse scheme.

> Small fauna
taking refuge in their cover, yielding food
when all else is depleted. Why is it, then,
in our street-wisdom, in our what-we-do mind,
we prefer a tendril of the exotic, the world
of orderliness?

Nature favors adaptation,
the ability to survive. When I grow weary,
bone-tired, of contention, I hike to the floe-river,
stand on its rocky bank, listen,
admire the stench of one maverick
stiff-needled seedling.

Early Walk, Late October

It resembles a cat or dog along the curb
from a distance under the lamp of moon as I cross
the footbridge over the broken-glass creek.

Closer, it's a doe, its rear legs wrenched beneath.
I suck in dark air, my ankles stiffen in their socks.
The string of traffic swerves, does not slow down.

Pawing her front legs, she struggles to lift the sack
of her body out of harm's way, her brown eyes
huge in the oncoming headlights. Nobody's fault.

How many times before, I think, she must have
chanced this clash of nature and development,
survived by the sheer luck of numbers. Late

October, and soon enough, the night will swell
with witches and brooms, clowns and monsters,
the chatter of youth, chill of the unknown.

There's nothing I can do: crush of tires,
her 200 pounds. I turn and run. Trailing me,
a human-like sound crying out from the wild.

Wild Turkey

We live in a rainbow of chaos.—Paul Cézanne

One of our largest birds—easy target—
yet it camps under scrub trees undisturbed
at creek's edge. At that hinge of order
and confusion, in a flock clustered between
a four-lane and the old city landfill.

We've watched this city accelerate, outgrow,
its concentric bands complicit with all
that is bland, like the meadow behind my yard,
once a stand of milo filled with bird song.
Why do we fear those orders not understood?

It thrives in a spectrum of common spaces
not easily rearranged, foraging.
Give me the fringe any day, the interface
where things wild flourish, an arc toward
the unfathomable. For now, we say, it is safe.

The dump continues its slow disintegration.
Tonight I'll step out my back door, take it all
in: sun in flames, hiss of tires, fall air on my neck
cooling. The black shells of bodies roosting,
meanwhile, untethered and just beyond.

Great Horned Owl

All afternoon, in chill northern gusts, yellowed leaves
fly silent off the oak. The windbreak shivers, the green
bowl of lawn holds its breath in anticipation.

Even without binoculars, the owl's bulk looks ominous
on the branch, its head swiveling side to side and down,
its sockets fixed, sweeping the nervous view.

From inside the house, I stare at ear tufts,
eye rings, hooked bill, flat disk of face, perching there
on dangerous talons, resting its great wing-feathers.

What must it be looking for, listening to? I wonder if it, too,
suffers from insomnia, awake during the day for no good
reason, if maybe like me it thinks as long as it's up

why not *do* something—late-day snack, say—there in the loft,
as if it's at a theater before the lights gradually dim, before
the main attraction, which I, too, sometimes switch on

late at night—the movie channel—huddled in down,
hungry, there in the dark focusing on those classic
figures so often bloodied in black and white.

Procrastination

The art of keeping up with yesterday.—Don Marquis

By December its face had collapsed into dark comedy:
exaggerated grin, loose teeth, nose and eye triangles
wrinkled inward, its insides a fungus among us,

no intention to leave the jack-o-lantern out there,
but after a while it became a fascination—not the putting off
or the act of carrying it back to the compost pile—

but the whole spectacle, the protracted rotting, cell
by broken cell, in January I watched it on the post from inside,
chewing a ham sandwich, sipping coffee, staring out

while the snow filled up, thinking of its icy insides, its deflating
air spaces, and yes, I gave it a rest, postponed the task
until better weather, deferred to atmosphere,

slowing the car, then, up the driveway, or dawdling
close to it on my way down to the mailbox, the faded crater
all through February hanging on by its very spines,

testimony to the genius of horticulture, this cousin to squash
and melons and cukes, known, I read somewhere,
as *pompion*, meaning cooked by the sun,

and when I look up, there it is: the sun, cerulean sky again,
the heavy bodies of geese on their return to Canada,
birds pecking away at its insides now, the dried seeds,

by March a breeze beckoning and I've stalled long enough,
I'll drag out my gardener's feet and what's left of that sorry
excuse for a vegetable I'll by god frisbee into the day.

Swiss Cheese

*Cheese makers want to loosen the regulation, put
a little flexibility in.*—Wisconsin Cheese Makers Assn.

When I read in the newspaper the Feds may change
the holes in Swiss cheese, I wonder: will they further coagulate
cottage cheese, jack around with my pepper jack?

I hate to think what further regulations we must be freed from.
I've been perfectly happy with those holes, thank you,
no self-respecting deli meal would be complete without.

But what do I know? Some folks can't stomach it, the stuff
of cows I recall feeding to the hogs. A friend asks, only half-
joking: if yogurt goes bad, how would you know?

Let's not confuse ourselves with facts: the holes
in Swiss cheese must change, and by god, we can count
on a Washington bureaucrat to look right into it.

Never mind tradition or antiquity or technology.
Never mind those farm policies that do actual harm.
After all, there's no such thing as a happy farmer.

Hey, thanks to Reagan and deregulation, I can't now
count on the airlines but can sometimes wear a size 6.
So why not walk on the wild side, go with the flow,

cut'em some slack and live it up. Downsize those holes
in the Swiss cheese—the sooner, the quicker. Let's see
if it'll wash in Wisconsin. Let's milk this for all it's worth.

Lettuce

A luxury once reserved for nobility,
    so esteemed any Greek slave caught eating it
        was given thirty lashes.

The Emperor Augustus regularly ate it
    at the end of a meal; later, Domitian
        would prefer it as an appetizer.

Today, early, step out to your garden
    and simply harvest, gathering proof
        that nature is benign and generous.

It's of the genus *Lactuca*, meaning milk,
    when cut losing milk-like juices, a later
        mild cousin to the wild prickly native.

Look under the leafy canopy where gnats
    and mosquitoes rest, where soil
        splatters upward from late night showers.

The plants rise delicate and tender
    from their composted beds, greens, reds,
        sweet, buttery, smooth, broad, frilly.

To eat leaf lettuce is to taste early summer,
    its pale colors, its temperatures,
        the earth, the air, the temporary rain.

Shredded Wheat

At the kitchen table with a box of cold cereal,
you read news of the world from the makers
of shredded wheat.

                Not bite-size, not frosted
or current-flavored, but petite pillows wrapped
in wax paper, and, if you're lucky, whole.
Is this the seed or the straw?

               Across the oilcloth
your older brother crushes his into a heaping haystack,
same as he crushes crackers over soup and builds volcanoes
on his supper plate of mashed potatoes, complete
with gravy magma, oozing.

               This is the brother
who balances on the flatbed behind the baler—Father
at the wheel of the John Deere—lifting and stacking haybales
with the business end of a metal hook.

              Both of you pour on sugar and milk—
whole and unpasteurized from a small herd munching
hay, corn, dust, each cow with its four amazing stomachs,
raw milk run through the separator, cream to the co-op,
skim to the hogs.

              By the time you reach the bottom,
the helping, no matter its size, is a soggy mess. Outdoors,
the world is a lively, dirt-filled farmyard with clouds overhead,
puffed and distant.

              If you are what you eat, this brother is pure
meat-and-potatoes muscle, father all egg and field corn
and dairy, all systems slowly clogging. But this news
you don't know right now, you just don't.

Green Apples

Because I want to be my older brother
I do what he tells me,
with saltshaker, in hand-me-downs,
climb behind him up a ladder of limbs

in the run-down orchard, perch at attention
on the opposite side of the trunk, await
orders: apples, tart, inside and out
the shade of early summer.

The newly feathered pullets, meanwhile,
beaks clipped, eyes blank, clucking
at random for cracked corn and oyster shells
in the dirt below, while

Mother gathers grocery money in the chicken house,
where the dust of feathers and straw and droppings
hangs visible in the air, a pungent haze,
where a few hens huddle over hope in cubicles.

When he says go, we lick and salt,
that first mouthful a bolt through the taste buds,
my brother and I cohorts in a conspiracy of silence.
With a pocket knife he stabs out worm holes,

and because I want to be my older brother
I bite and spit, hoping this will do the trick,
unlock the door to the secret clubhouse, whether in
the attic or on boards nailed into a branch,

notion to be blunted sooner rather than later,
this brother betraying me when my stomach rebels,
knuckles punching my arm silly, Mother saying
if I told you once I told you a thousand times,

there in a tangle of leaves, in a land of feast and famine,
among pears and feeder calves, pines and manure,
sweet clover and silage, under the indifferent farmyard sun
where for a brief lifetime my brother and I were one.

Pastoral

I see myself on the dusty farmstead in handed-down denims,
clutching a hairless doll, watching my young older brother.

The air is thick with summer, the wind laden with topsoil,
around us discarded implements, rusted fence-wire, ragweed.

He's shinnied up a silver maple and knocked down his prize,
his boredom-fighter: the grass-and-feather nest of sparrows.

I am unable to speak up, to articulate what is wrong or right.
In that sweaty afternoon I watch him take aim, wind up

his best overhand, fling one after another new hatchlings—
small smackings—against the back of the empty brooder house.

Soon he will spend untold hours on a tractor in the fields.
Why does darkness haunt me, what can I gain from it now?

***

Death was there, always, reminding us often of its presence.
Cattle and hogs were bred, then fed, solely for slaughter.

Chickens for the egg money, for their wholesale fryer-weight.
Those, plus field grain, providing our food, our subsistence.

Stillborns and disease and accidents took their toll, robins'
eggs dropping to the ground, even our own pets non-exempt.

But then I was only a girl, ingesting black earth and blue sky,
listening with my eyes, breathing fear and helplessness.

Fall would soon shove summer aside, snow to slam hard
into the windbreak, spring migrating back again on mud feet.

If fledglings strengthened their wings and flew off, could I?
I felt the sun burn, watched a cat lurch for the half-limp form.

Saga

Viking clash: Danes and Swedes battle
to be biggest.—news article, Europe

They're still at it, waging battles worthy of a Viking
headline some ten centuries later, those northern
legendaries who stormed sea and land by boat.

Stockholm has declared itself the Capital of
Scandinavia. Copenhagen responded, flexing
muscle, attempting to retake its 16th-century trademark.

And it seems IKEA, the furniture giant, uses Swede
names for its shiniest, comfiest furnishings while Danish
towns are relegated to doormats, rugs, and carpets.

No accident, according to one critic. "It is exactly 350 years
since Swedes took the Halland, Skåne and Blekinge regions
from Denmark." Demographic lessons die hard.

Raiders with style, the Vikings turned out to be
technologists ahead of their time, builders of sophisticated
ships and towns, and not just bear-skinned *berserkers*.

But with all those fjords and feuds between them, who can
blame one or the other for claiming Odin to be on his side?
As it happened in this country, too, late 19th century,

when my Dane grandfather registered for citizenship
at the county courthouse, the Swede clerk entered
granddad's name ending in "son" instead of "sen."

Half a world from their homelands, the Swede shrugged,
said it didn't matter, while at his mercy Hans Peter Wilhelm
Paulsen knowing *blødende* well it did.

Work

*The honeybee can fly nearly 5 billion miles
on one gallon of honey.* —NPR news

On spring days you could hear it—
buzzing cloud back and forth between fencerow
and hives, over the rugosa roses and the field,
forty acres of clover with its billions of tiny blooms.

My father grinned as he opened a top, brushed aside
the bodies, pried out a frame oozing with sweetness,
my hands on the extractor handle sticky with the great
efficiency and substance of their labor.

Worker bees, like my farmer father, combed those fields
for a harvest of gold. Some years crop failure and bad luck
weather affected supply and yield. All that labor translated
into a meager existence, a tightening of the belts.

Worker bees kick out the drones to protect their winter food.
Back then, all we needed was whatever we raised, planted,
butchered and preserved. There were no guarantees.
We took care of the land; the land took care of us.

All honeybees need is pollen and nectar, an unspoiled spring-
fed creek, the occasional gentle hand to encourage them on.

Returning to St. Louis, Lewis and Clark See a Cow

two-and-a-half years after departure, their expedition
almost complete, floating downstream on the muddy Mo,
the cow maybe in now what is known as Nebraska,

near my home town, perhaps, six miles from there
on rolling hills of rich loam that would later yield
with little resistance to settlement and plow, natives pushed

aside, that cow their icon of modern civilization, after months
and discovery of the previously undocumented, trekking into
the unknown, failing to find the passage yet not failing,

living by their wits and the kindnesses of the unwitting,
if they had died along the journey it would have been only
delayed, this dream—destiny—signaling for many downfall,

that cow they cheered at, not as product or commodity,
but the genuine article, cow munching grass stamped indelible
into their gray matter as it surely was in mine, my future built

on top of so many cowhides, carved from those fields,
the slash and boom and bust out on that temperate plain, way
of life that has almost died, one cow shuffling after the other

on the recent-worn path, their triumph, that temporary success.

A Farm Story

He unlocks the cabinet before dawn,
before the bulk of his fellow workers arrive.
In the cooled-down air he removes his knives,
palms the wood handles and begins sharpening,
a rapid-arm motion of metal on metal,
standing in sawdust, odor of grease
everywhere thick.

Do not pity him.
It is not a scandal to wish a different life
for your sons, to be the generation
that escapes the debt of the land.

Sides of beef wait on hooks in the cooler.
Today he will carve flesh and bone
like they taught him in Toledo,
wielding the day for wages,
his wrists stiffening.
Tomorrow is the Fourth of July.
He is almost sixty.

Later he will flash his wife a grin,
recline into an evening of easy chair.
Outdoors, humid air will settle
on ungrazed grass.

My Father's War

Not the first one he was too young for
not Iwo Jima   Anzio   the death march of Bataan
one of our neighbors survived   my father by accident

of birth caught between the war to end all wars
and the greatest generation   his on-going battle
to farm instead of finishing high school

exempt from service   worked our hilled
acres with two-row and four-bottom   manure
and rotation   eking out an ever-shrinking cut

Natives meanwhile on the nearby reservation
on some of the steepest hills in this state   some
drunk on government dole   punched holes in walls

of their cheap government houses   flickering reels
replayed pow-wows   the girl in leather dress jingles
Does her spirit rustle above the grass at Blackbird Hill

Like his flat-footed father who left the homeland
to escape hardship   the king's army conscription
my father could see the writing in the ag bill

government dole   mostly for corporate benefit
D.C. pundits urging to get big or get out
so it was decided for us   to leave   to escape

I wonder what might have become of that girl
on the grass dancing   is she still alive
her people driven off their hunting grounds

And the other one   looking back   no escape
those modest acres not far from Blackbird Hill
her spirit rising above the everyday ravage of the land

Greasy Spoon

In a small town, in a dark-paneled café called Harold's
at a plastic-topped table, I sit with my mother and her sisters.

They debate roast beef or chicken, sandwich or dinner special,
coffee or just water. I scan the menu for anything of redemption,

keep my expectations low. They're getting up there in years.
I study lined faces, veined hands, clean-your-plate waistlines.

It's noon, and the place overflows—feed salesmen, bankers,
retirees—folks who, my aunt says, like to eat what others cook.

I think of these sisters, their grins in the sepia portrait—bobbed hair,
best Sunday dresses—the handsome family gazing out at a world

before the Great Depression, before they lived an uncertain future,
no guarantee for that next meal. We would have starved to death

if not for our grandparents, my aunt says. Mother adds, They
gave us a chicken for the eggs, but we had to eat the chicken, too.

Now, you might not guess: my mother's bent shoulders, one aunt's
unsteady hand, the other with excess pounds to lug around.

Their dinners arrive on oval platters: meat, potatoes, a layer of gravy,
rolls and over-cooked vegetables. This is plenty, I insist, pointing

to my wedge of lettuce and watery soup. When they were young,
their options were limited; they kept their expectations low. Now

they relish each pleasant surprise fate happens to dish out.
We're all from a long line of the common, the ordinary, the land;

some lessons you never outgrow. On mother's recent ocean cruise,
what she enjoyed most was the food: four complete dining rooms!

Woman who has lugged around her first electric range, since 1952,
from farm to city; it now resides in her basement. Never know

when you might need an extra oven. These sisters don't dwell
on the past. Our waitress stops by, my aunt winks. Pie, anyone?

Refractions

Some day she hopes her timing is right—
staring west just as the sun disappears
below the curvature of earth—sunlight in all its wave-
lengths scattering down the vertical spectrum
into a green rare flash.

* * *

Twinkle, twinkle: dotting the night sky starlight
fluctuates into flicker, bent by earth's atmosphere—
the way a straw appears to bend in a glass of water—
a swirling of warm, cold, dry, moist, dense and less dense
air: what you see is not necessarily what you get.

* * *

And not exactly *objects are closer than they appear*
as in the car mirror, but curve of the eyeball causing
images to focus in front of, instead of on, the retina:
myopia, the world turning fuzzy, a young child
singing the nursery rhyme, nibbling, sniffing

* * *

possibilities, her flawed vision apparent later,
after her father walked her down the lane to look up
at the Big Dipper she couldn't see, until after
the thick eyeglasses, the arc of years, the hurried
sunsets, her winking father gone in such a flash.

After a Rain

After a rain I yank weeds in the flowerbed—crabgrass and foxtail,
the usual suspects—and because moisture is abundant, seedlings

of maple and ash, my own private forest, which undeniably multiplies
beneath the windbreak I planted years ago, where, thanks to birds,
scores of young cedar, mulberry, wild cherry now tangle. For now

I concentrate on these out of place plants that arrived by airwaves
last season, graceful, on their single- and double-winged samaras.

As a child, I welcomed those helicopters, gathered them
and climbed to the height of the windmill to send a bucketful twirling
toward the gravel farm yard, my own private landing strip.

And Father recalling the Dirty Thirties, years when heat and drought
ganged up, searing young crops in fields, turning them white overnight.

Today, I count blessings: cool air, a rainbow of blooms, damp earth.
Even rain gutters unattended sprout things, leafy and green. Would
father grin at my yard, its overly dense and grandiose scheme?

Birds at the feeder make a joyful noise. I stand up, light-headed, giddy.
If I spread my arms, I could more or less abandon myself to the wind.

Small

When I was small, we made s'mores,
but don't bother looking that one up.

We were small fry in a small town, making small
talk about small-time lives into the small hours.

I was often forced to sing small after my older brother
made me feel very, very small. Older brothers are good

at that. I was good at typing, pounding out one-hundred-
ten correct words of small pica per minute in class,

the small roar of clackety-clack and carriage returns,
my best friend and I in a small but undeclared race.

We were insignificant and small potatoes, but were we
small-minded? It was our teacher, petite and blonde

Miss Buskirk, who also taught home ec and shorthand,
who made us notice. Mr. Kahler, our science and math

teacher, when they met in the hall, the small sparks between
them. Her smile a pearly dazzle, his the perfect small-boy

grin. All that fall, the young new teachers in our small high school,
we watched it grow. At homecoming, then, on a slow dance,

his hand on the small of her back. Back then we didn't know
squat, but this, we just knew this would lead to something big.

Egg

Dazzling array, endless possibilities—
scrambled, fried, poached, soft or hard—this ovum
of the chicken reliable as the spring full moon,
and there in the refrigerator door a resurrected taste:

after chores a brother, slouched over his plate, carving bacon;
on the oilcloth a sister arranging and rearranging a quilt
of broken shell fresh from the brooder house, where
earlier her hand stole into straw beneath cluck and feather;

a father in oil-stained overalls; forever a mother
in the farm kitchen cleaning chickens, where sometimes
a soft-formed egg would fall out from those ropey innards.
For now, I set aside these souvenirs.

Which came first? The egg to ancients a sacred symbol:
shell of earth, white of water, yolk of fire. In this cell of city air
I now take these elements—swirling and simmering—
another mortal turning a small miracle into lunch.

Bird

Some days I see it more than I wish: wax outline on my window
the perfect shape of bluejay, replete with bits of feather.

Breast feathers splayed, outer primaries curved, extended,
orbitals surrounding eyes as if to defy the laws of aerodynamics.

I feed them, invite that other kingdom into my living room, blind
to my transparent and unforgiving scheme. Whose fault?

Back in the 50s, my father scoffed at a neighbor's remodeling—
new picture window—why in the world would you always wish to see

the land where you spend your waking hours? My mother trying her best
to drive away the grit of soil, the bawl and cluck of livestock, the smell.

Those days oriole nests hung pendulous in elms, robin eggs broke in mud,
my brother flung baby sparrows into a pail, stuck in the labyrinth of youth.

I keep trying to erase these shadows, that evidence. Perhaps too close
to the sun once, twice, my feathers disappeared: I no longer dream of flying.

Opossum

Mostly they belong to the night, to the dull-orange eye-shine
out of the thicket, short legs scurrying over dry leaves.

Today, it waddles across the back yard to the deck for a drink
from the birds' water dish, bringing its legends: my father

telling how his mother chased one from the henhouse,
with a shovel hit it into dirt, bleeding from its mouth, then,

until she returned to the house only to see it limp off
down the lane. Survival and adaptation and success, this

primitive pouch-mammal through the millennia unchanged:
built low, slow, clumsy paws, pink toes and bony tail,

fur coarse and of little monetary value. That snout only
a mother could love. So close now I can almost touch it,

the possum, his face all grin and eyes blue sky, my father
and his faded stories long since gone from my grasp.

Swallows

I step lightly on to the footbridge,
  trying to imagine all the lives
    underneath.

Below: swift brown water.
  Above, and through the fence:
    swallows—cliff swallows—a colony

rollercoasting the damp cool air,
  clattering and soaring en masse,
    perfectly suited to human structures.

Their adaptation brings to mind
  the ancient ones, the hollowed-out
    cliff dwellings, how once in winter

I crawled inside, earth
  and slant of sun warming me,
    a place, perhaps, to grow up safe.

And my own grandfather, early settler
  on the Plains, living in a summer dugout
    along Bell Creek, breaking sod.

So many animals dwelling therein;
  adobe—clay and grass—made
    by humans for untold years.

Now I work to focus on one swallow:
  throat patch, square tail, rusty rump,
    mouth wide for capturing insects.

One after another they dive along the bank
  into mud, then head beneath me, building
    their jug-nests, returning to that place

we call home.

Leap of Faith

Billions of insects pass unseen over your head in a summer month.
—NPR news

So when the scientist said there's an invisible herd of animal life
several thousand feet up in the air, I immediately clammed up.

Not that outdoors I was in immediate danger of swallowing them—
not like the summer I inhaled a swarm of gnats while whizzing down

the dirt hill on two wheels toward Bell Creek yards behind my brother,
who once had the misfortune of a bee sting inside his ear. No, it's more

like what else, what else could possibly be humming just outside
our awareness, beyond our own invisible shell? Just think: billions

of insects overhead, billions of stars in our galaxy, the untold number
of angels dancing somewhere unseen. Not much comfort knowing we share

sixty percent of our genes with bananas. We know carnage on the windshield
at 75 mph driving I-80 in summer, but bugs riding high? Pilots know. Even

Charles Lindbergh collected them at 5,000 and 12,000 feet on flights across
the Atlantic. A live termite was captured at 19,000 feet. A matter of survival,

they say, for space and food and sex: bugs launch themselves into the wind,
a leap of faith. Remember that dream as a kid, the feeling when you spread

your arms and could fly? Every child is an artist; the problem is how to remain
one. Back then, I watched with envy as my brother swung wired hay from

the business end of the baler by hook, stacked bales neat and swift on the trailer,
pure symmetry, muscle, motion, my summers spent inside a book. Where

does it go, all that ability, buried desire, unused metaphor, the collective art
that elevates us from all creation? Suppose it bubbles into the troposphere,

drifts on surface winds so that on my walk—today, for example—I breathe a billion inventions from those before, filter the collective past swirling

through cloud and insect, steal what rides the airwaves into my own hive of the invisible as it billows toward the distant and unknowable stars.

Autumn

I walk west before dawn, shiver at the sight of lightning,
at clouds dark in the distance eclipsing a full harvest moon.

Autumn: Earth tipping on its axis, Northern Plains spiraling
into the fermented season, creek a bulge on its tireless race

to the river. No rumbling yet, just tires on pavement, wind howling
a strong case: *walk fast, walk fast, before your bones turn to ash.*

What keeps it all alive? At least I'm not alone: on concrete
a dictionary of motion—ants, crickets, sow bugs—in their constant

unfinished calling, others in grass stroking their waterproof shells.
Just before the rain drops, I turn my back to thunder, face a sky

trying its best, turning yellow-pink, east light diffused and artsy,
and speed up, past the void of fields going surely green to gold.

Early December

Clear dark sky before dawn,
sun a vivid dream below the horizon.

She speed-walks west along Superior Street,
to the southeast the moon a wry smile and Venus'
unblinking eye like a doting father.

The sharp air tastes of earth beneath a coat
of frost, the wind stings; silent wings and stilt-legs
glide away from her over the glass creek.

She knows it's out here, beside the stubblefields
and traffic, as always, the face of love and beauty.

The dome of early morning goes lighter
above the bliss and rush of the everyday,
the blue that has long been her favorite.

She is the lone figure walking at this hour in the cold.
She will always be the girl out walking.

Leap Second

It is absolutely not because of tidal forces. The newspaper
reports a leap second will be added at the end of the year.

I hold the paper with one hand, the other one falling asleep
under the full weight of a three-year-old, her brown hair

matted from fever, her head resting in the hollow
between breast and arm. We breathe in unison.

A good thing, I think: time slowing down, this simple
and absolutely necessary thing called healing.

Long ago my own burrowing into father's chair after chores,
the *World-Herald* in his leathery hands, his face washed,

the lingering aroma of grease and livestock and sweat.
My towhead resting in the crook of his arm. The news

then in a pre-nuclear age, before the dawn of precise
atomic clocks. Time then when time seemed endless.

Astronomers claim it's necessary—the leap second—
to sync with Earth's rotation, somewhat unreliable.

Times then when I lay on the sofa, sick, imagining
shapes, all manner of things, twirling on a plaster ceiling.

In the long run will we notice? A good thing, I decide:
arm and finger and knee twitching into dreamland, one

extra moment to our lives, this planet's passage—
at fourteen miles a second—around the sun.

My Granddaughter Sick

All day the house as if holding its breath.

I kiss the top of her fevered head,
her hair fine as milkweed fluff,

delicate like chick down. Meanwhile
the moon, a heavy saucer, reclines

pale and cumbersome above the treeline,
this chilled horizon brittle with bare limbs.

She sleeps, earth moving on its tiptoes,
planets on their unblinking vigil.

Out on the lake, ice pings and twangs
its thick, hard-water blues. By morning

there will be a shift in the jet stream,
an upswing of wind clean out of the south.

Birds will tweet a brighter tune; once
again, the quick red fox will dart to safety.

Shadows

Early morning, my shadow tracks ahead of me
across the sidewalk, resembling the stick-and-circle
person my granddaughter draws—bulbous torso,
exaggerated spindle-legs, tiny head, wild
morning hair

                     dry spring, drier winter,
sandbars lifting higher out of the creekbed,
dust off new developments blowing up
a brown windstorm over the highway

        we could really use some rain
        we could really use some rain

                       in the nearby field
a spray rig with oversized tires, its tiny cab
and skinny boom-arms fully extended strides
the arid land like some mutated dragonfly,
spewing chemicals into the wind,
and you wonder

        we could really use some rain
        we could really use

                   and you keep on going,
which is all any shadow can do, one foot
then the other, trying not to feel useless,
taking it all in

        we could really
        really

                              the wind—
over mouse-eared chickweed in a failed lawn,
its pungent odor rising, or through last year's
spent cattails, the call of a redwing blackbird,
rattling.

Relativity

Self-evident: time was simpler when recorded
by phases of the moon, as Cro-Magnons did, or
as animals know by sun and season, day and night.

Calendars were created by human need for predictability,
clocks calibrated now to a precise number of atom
vibrations. Thank those early astronomers, their curiosity
as they contemplated the vast and flickering universe.

Now, we all know time is money, the time is now, now
is the only time we have. But, does anybody really know?
Time and space, Einstein reminds us, are relative.

Take this silver pocket watch, its back worn to brass,
face cracked, its crystal badly scratched. Rattled about
the pocket of my father's work jeans in fields and barns,
those seesaw years of dust and heat and howling snow.

Unwound in my desk drawer, it's neither here nor there.
All is relative in this invented environment. Wristwatches,
for example, weren't popular until WWI aviators needed them.

When the young child, learning her big and little hands,
asks me What time is it, I gather her up, go outdoors to study
leaf and sky, the mysteries of green and blue, the dozen
or so timepieces in my house running wild beyond belief.

Taking the Young Child

I take the young child to see the blossoms:
four-direction openings of the pure white cross—

Cornus. She is only three, yet she knows of gift,
rises on her tiptoes to inhale it. But of suffering?

The pain of storms, covering my ears when branches
twist and fall from unseasonable weather. Oh

dogwood of the southern hardwood forests, I worry
over your misplaced finery, your tender display.

The young child, without hesitation, gathers each
bloom—lilac, tulip, viburnum—imprinting spring.

Her eyes are hazel, lips a cupid rose, hair the silk
of maplewood, her face the flower I bend to kiss.

Sleep

Adult: I have trouble falling asleep at night.
Child: But don't you close your eyes?

The art of sleep isn't tough for those who have the gift—
they're puzzled at the rest of us with trouble in the night.

And during the day, that tumbling sensation, anxious, sad,
the blues, the sun slipping low beyond our grasp.

Tossing and taking forever, we conjure the ancient ones
whose lives revolved around the same sun—sun worshipers—

who discovered fire, calculated the heavens, tracked stars,
who likely slept through most of this gloomy season.

We can't help but wonder how they'd react to light—
fake light—the stuff we do to trick our body-clock

into believing we are more than some grand experiment—
superior, in fact—to the pull of nature, however quaint.

It's all we can do to force ourselves out the door in the dark,
overcome the urge to curl into a book and hibernate.

And that child—remember? how we tiptoed not to wake—
a now impossible teen in all her tough circadian torpor.

Perfection

In nature, nothing is perfect and everything is perfect.
Trees can be contorted, bent in weird ways,
and they're still beautiful. —Alice Walker

In the newspaper I learn that 43,000 year-old Neanderthal
bones were found to contain the language gene.
This warms me somehow, as I tread the bike trail

on a cold morning in November, strange comfort to think
that our long-ago relatives, too, had the gift of gab,

advanced perhaps as those swell clicks of instant text,
small gifts from the adolescent. In a gated, complicated world,
what can I possibly say to claim attention from cyberspace,

of slow heron wings in tandem, churning, tilting, the sunrise copper,
of leaves gold letting go one at a time, exposing the large-boned

and twisted bark on the bur oak, of the mudded creek that
musters my earlier days, insatiable, of cottonwoods and cattle
and field crops to harvest, the long sequence of stories that have led

both of us here, now? She won't listen. Youth wasted on the young?
As in trees and in language, a beautiful thing is never perfect.

Surely Neanderthals adapted, related tales of their own survival.
The long-ago storyteller in me twitches; I am tireless but to try.
Besides, isn't perfection overrated? Let's get it roughly right.

My Husband's Grandmother Worked for Willa Cather

That was the legend, a string
of stories passed down while she still lived:
sailed alone at age twelve from Ireland,
lived with sisters in New York until they quarreled,
boarded a train for Nebraska, then,

alighted in her elegant threads
and plumed hat at Red Cloud, all 4'10"
of her oozing sophistication, the carpenter-farmer
falling for her at first sight. Copper-haired
Kitty and hammer-man Henry, marrying.

And this is where the tablet goes fuzzy,
the classic immigrant tale turns cryptic:
devout Catholic, four children in four years,
he dies. Apparently she does what she can:
cook, wash, scrub, dust, haul ash.

I met her as the white-haired matriarch,
her brogue thick and intact, her green eyes afire.
She worked for the Cathers; this much is true.
Only on that first day it seems when told
she must remove her plate from the dining room,

Kitty—God I love it!—turned on her heels,
strode through the swinging kitchen door
where lunch simmered on the stove, became
the servant girl who walked from that story
clean out the back door.

Bread

Like snowflakes, no two loaves look exactly
alike. Not when they are made of elements—
flour, leavening, liquid—not when the hands
that form them are human and therefore flawed.

The story of gluten, from a grass—wheat—from
the Middle East and prehistoric. The language
of texture and crumb, a simple unspoken act
of union—the making, breaking of bread.

On a Saturday this breadwinner might be up
to his elbows slap-happy, kneading, bringing forth
to feed our small multitude. Hands stirring, punching,
greasing, shaping. Man who all week swims up-

stream, numb from the intangible, now surrendering
to process. I watch his arms, his shoulders, his
whole body moving to a rhythm old as man,
tuned to these ingredients, this given atmosphere.

An act of faith, plunging into dough, giving it life,
the magic of yeast, sacrament of earth. The laying
of hands over the rising and plump, hands that later—
take, eat—will surely quicken other pliable mounds.

The house in anticipation inhales, exhales. Give us this
day; we have decided, for now, not to die—not yet.
And when it comes hot from the oven, we sit down
to behold! the miracle: each bite holy on the tongue.

The Cardinal

Dum spiro, spero.—Ovid

The heart does not easily give up.
Late fall, berries gone, bare limbs
corkscrew in daylight.

                 I watch him
from the shell of my wing-back chair,
his insistent charge toward glass.

Day into day, the thump and hover,
his own ticker-tape parade of one.
Birds have been flying

                 blind into
these windows for years, but this—
a warning, crimson spirit, spurned lover?

On days I don't see him, I worry.
This is my life: don't thumb it away.
But what would I say to this masked man,

this Royal Canadian Mounted Police
in pointed hat, Lone Ranger riding Silver
on wings?

             It's as if he's sneaking me
a message—carrier pigeon in uniform,
beak tapping politely on the glass—

clinging, peering in:
as long as I breathe, I hope.

Feeding the Hawk

I do this on a warm afternoon, June,
from a chaise on the deck, my hand
holding a glass: wine, red, and

overhead a splay of tail to match,
above the back tree line, above
the field beyond; the hawk soars,
ignores the jays and chatter.

I am feeding the hawk one small
rodent or mammal at a dive,
creatures that roam my land

in search of worm or grub or root,
below the tangle of branch and limb
and trunk, leaf and needle and
blade, flower and pollen and sap,

where feathers and fur and
claws small enough attempt
to disappear when wings cast

their shadow, ripple through heat,
rising, tilt outstretched, still.
It's as if this slow moment
is a shower of manna, a sign.

On command, I take, eat, drink
in ethereal communion with the gods.

July

All day from the grove a chorus of cicadas.
In the distance, a thunderstorm flashes

over the city through evening clouds,
and one by one lightning bugs

signal their luminous abdomens
to the opposite sex. A hot wind

pumping humidity across the low hills,
into the trembling leaves of cottonwood.

July: crabgrass setting plump seedheads,
tomatoes bending under green loads,

a plains toad staking its cool claim
under the dog's water dish.

Somewhere in this composed suburb
a couple will switch off their reading lamps

and turn in the gathering dark to face
each other. Out in a farmer's cornfield

heated leaves will gradually unfold,
admitting their heavenly gifts.

Remembrance

After the threat of storm in the distance,
after music, after the words *war* and *a-bomb*
and *remembrance*, I can't help but wonder:
where are they now, the spirits of those long gone?

In a few days I'll be sitting on a prairie hilltop,
hoping to glimpse the August meteor shower,
the Perseids, after Perseus who beheaded Medusa,
her demon eye still winking at us from the heavens.

How many stories does it take to explain everything:
the snake-haired monster with gaze that turned people
to stone, the coyotes that dance among the stars and
sometimes streak-fall from the sky, a man-made force

that rained down death for thousands, fear for us all?
For now, we do what the living sometimes do best:
craft messages of hope, mingle in the magic of dusk,
let loose fragile lanterns that float away on water.

August 12 in the Nebraska Sand Hills Watching the Perseids Meteor Shower

In the middle of rolling grasslands, away from lights,
a moonless night untethers its wild polka-dots,
the formations we can name competing for attention
in a twinkling and crowded sky-bowl.

Out from the corners, our eyes detect a maverick meteor,
a transient streak, and lying back toward midnight
on the heft of car hood, all conversation blunted,
we are at once unnerved and somehow restored.

Out here, a furrow of spring-fed river threads
through ranches in the tens of thousands of acres.
Like cattle, we are powerless, by instinct can see
why early people trembled and deliberated the heavens.

Off in the distance those cattle make themselves known,
a bird song moves singular across the horizon.
Not yet 2:00, and bits of comet dust, the Perseids,
startle and skim the atmosphere like skipping stones.

In the leaden dark, we are utterly alone. As I rub the ridges
on the back of your hand, our love for all things warm
and pulsing crescendos toward dawn: this timeless awe,
your breath floating with mine upward into the stars.

Early Winter

Last night the sharp slice of moon
poured down its milk.
Not in the forecast, but there it was, liquid
and jiggly suspended over the front lawn,
as long as you stood silent, drank it all in.

In the light of day—no sign of it—
brown leaves and bared limbs,
the littered ground after a long season,
only the grassblades carrying a residue
of off-white. Odd and fickle,

this landscape of the heart.
And yet: breathe in the late afternoon sun,
feel it warm the geraniums of summer
on the windowsill, fuchsia and rose and salmon
flirting back, their shameless love.

Driving West Ireland in Winter

On a clear day, you're tempted
to convert—rain, sun, rainbow
enough to complement gold—

driving the wrong side on highways
barely adequate for one,
walls and vines, hugging the edge,

with few directions and fewer signs,
you pray and stop three times to ask,
and by miracle you find yourself

pulling on a Guinness at the pub,
first a shot then this peat-infused food
that sustains you from village to village,

where landscape and literature converge,
where cliff and rock and bog charm you
into small and disproportionate distances.

While gazing at moss-covered headstones
a thick-brogue voice calls, Want to see
the church? and you let her, caretaker

who rubs this site's carved rune-stone,
and it begins to sink in: a peopled land,
centuries, ancient walls and war lords,

and they all welcome you—inn and pub
and shop—curious why you're here
in this weather, the sign "Music Tonight"

meaning rock & roll, not fiddle, tourists
not here in numbers now, the sign facing
the other way warning Do Not Drive

When Flooded after you inch your way
through the water, praying, stopping
while sheep move from one pasture

to the next, taking the scenic road,
which is to say any road, leading you
to salt, to faith, to where it all began.

Solstice, December

Today, a few lucky travelers to Ireland
County Meath for seventeen minutes
Will witness a narrow beam of sun
Deep inside a chamber mound,
Same as its builders 4,000 years ago.

Try to imagine those ancient ones,
Months preparing for the long dark,
Storing food, scrounging fuel,
Not certain of survival.

They marked mid-winter
When the sun stands still,
Beseeched rebirth of the light,
Their fear it would not return
To bring another harvest.

Now we know it's just an
Astronomical position, an instant, sun
On the horizon at its lowest arc,
Most of us assured of another meal.

Overhead, the longest night aligns
The three stars of Orion's belt
With Sirius, brightest star in the east,
To mark where sun will rise
Late on the morning after.

Meanwhile, what northerners must
Do is carry on with decorative greens,
Deliberate fires, feasts like pagans
To celebrate year's cold end.

Near the Platte

On a wooded trail
the small waterfall is half frozen,
half emptying its bucket
over the edge of ancient plate rock,
the exposed formation in hills
that ancient people roamed,
gathering sticks and branches fallen
for their communal fire,
their luck of bounty and nomadic ritual.
Standing near it, we breathe snowmelt
and slight breeze, while overhead
the sun hides behind a layer of cloud.
We've had more than our share
this winter, we complain.
When will it ever end, we ask.
Later, back at the cabin,
we clink glasses, toast
the soreness of muscles, the red
of cheeks, the rip and roar
of logs now all warmth and flame.
The fact that we are here, alone
together, liquid flowing
freely from bottle and tap,
our ritual gathering and communion
homage to those before us, nomad
and immigrant and parent, lucky, our
lives blessed, eyes filling with smoke.

New Year's on Nine-Mile Prairie

Clouds in long rolls above the prairie hold promises
they can't keep. We walk in perennial tracks over
complicated tangles, eons of roots, an affinity of grasses
lying together, the ritual breathing of earth.

On the hilltop an elemental snap shot
nibbles at the gamut; winter the gaunt equalizer.
Solitude whistles through empty nest boxes,
around each chain link of the heart.

We are guests at a muslin tablecloth, served up sepia
seed heads under the forgiving distance of blue sky.
Alone together in the grace of resolution and celebration—
our gifts to each other—toward imperfect beginnings.

Two:
Linda M. Hasselstrom

—for Cora, Mildred, Josephine

I Ain't Blind and This is What I Think I See

Today I drive the Interstate, singing
rock and roll songs loudly, headed for
eastern South Dakota. I'm being paid
to teach a class or two, read poetry,
talk about the writing life.
I watch the borrow pit, bursting
with the smashed detritus from Dakota's winter.
No one knows exactly where I am.
I'm off the radar, lost inside the zone
where dead deer go, seeing everything
askew, surveying junk that winter
borrowed from the passersby.

At the corner of my eye
I see a dead raccoon cocooned
with coils of audio tape. A snowdrift
blackened by the spoils of winter
melts against the winds of spring.
"Neither a borrower nor a lender be,"
my father used to say, and then intone
another line: "For loan oft loses both
itself and friend." Is that an axle?
An Evinrude is heeled into the dirt;
a studded tire wrapped around a deer.
A hawk ascends and soars,
eyeing paper cartons hopping
like discarded Easter rabbits,
banks off to hunt for game
with blood and sinew,
flesh and bone.

At every mile of borrow ditch
I wonder if I'm seeing what I think
I see. A lava lamp. A stuffed bear.
A propeller. Silver CD discs shine

beside a license plate from Florida.
This rubble spells catastrophe
in every mile; spells loss.
A painted china tea set like
the one I had when I was three sits
beside a dead calf. My mother took
the photo as I shared my tea with Georgia,
the doll with yellow braided hair
who was my only friend.

Isn't that my other father
waving bye-bye as he did when I was
five? He's holding that same whiskey glass
he carried in the pictures
of my party. How fortunate we found
the borrowed dad who quoted
Shakespeare to me. Now I recall the rest:
"This above all: to thine own self
be true." A bumper sticker on a strip
of chrome advises me to DO IT NOW!

Two tail lights and the fender from
a 1954 Bel Air, the car I drove
to high school, lie beside
the fat guy from New York who said
I couldn't be a poet.
For every mile of borrow ditch:
more borrowed time,
more promise lost.

Bombing Again

Again the president—
a different one this time—
crouches behind his shield of office.
His empty desk shines.

We are defending ourselves,
he repeats,
against future attacks.
We have good reasons.
Smiling, he describes how our planes
dropped out of the sun
bearing our mother's sons,
dropped black bombs
out of the sun
onto the sons
of other mothers,
for good reason.

Again the long-faced commentators
analyze and point to maps,
long words tumbling
from their solemn faces.
In the snarl of words,
their fear is almost invisible.

Again I stand before my students,
listen to them say how well
they will do the job
that must be done,
how bravely they will defend their country,
No; of course they are not afraid.
Once more, we know everything
because we've watched it on TV,
and after all, they have it coming.
so we can eat our dinners
and sleep soundly
again.

Beltane, Reservation High School

Today the writer visits
a classroom on the reservation.
Facing the teenage heirs
of Crazy Horse and Sitting Bull,
I back against the chalkboard
to tell them that tonight
I'll join a group of white women
for a May Day rite
older than the oldest can recall.
One by one we'll walk a path
that snakes among the trees.
We'll reach a clearing where
one young pine tree stands alone,
and sing as we tie ribbons on the tree.
I write the colors on the board:
yellow stands for east, the region
of the mind, red for fire and spirit;
blue for water and the west,
and white for north and flesh we wear.
Singing we will circle, wheel and dip,
weaving colors, a net of prayer.

No one looks at me.
Outside the window I can see
across this dusty flat
the Black Hills blue with distance.
I know we all remember
the history we share.
Their fathers still say
that mine stole those far off hills
from tribes who call them sacred;
from tribes who want them back.

Tonight descendants
of the men who lied to Crazy Horse

will leave their living rooms,
their families and TV sets.
On sacred ground we'll call out
Celtic names old as eternity.
We'll stamp and whirl
and carry burning sage and sweetgrass.
Some of us will leave tobacco,
call the names of spirits
known to the Lakota,
known to the children in this room.

The tree we'll honor with our rites
chokes and shrivels in the ashy air.
Downhill, poisoned water flows
from the coiled heart of a spring
defiled with cyanide. The earth
on which we'll dance already quivers
to the bulldozer's mighty stride.

The students stare. I have stood
in silence much too long.
Write, I say, about worship.
Which beings fill you with awe?
What do you believe? What do you fear?

Every head turns as we look outside
where a white cross
cleaves blue air.

One Afternoon in a Reservation Classroom

The rat in the glass box
sleeps in his food dish,
forgetting the brown hands.
Dewey is exploring gravity:
how far back can he tip his desk
without falling over?
Jim talks Lakota to the room
grinning because the poet doesn't understand.
His eyes reveal his theme: "I hate you whites."

Marvin wrote six lines,
said "I'm done," and folded his hands.
I think he's asleep.
Blanche lies on her back on the floor,
legs sprawling,
says she can't think any other way.
Two teachers who sent their students home
are studying Spanish, loudly reciting
to each other in the final row.
Tisi and Debbie gossip about last night's party,
how drunk their mothers were.

Now Dewey discovers the earth's
vast power in the instant of defeat,
smacking his head on the floor.
Holding his stomach,
he lies on his back laughing.
Junior whispers to me
that he was praying when he made
the winning basket last night.
"Lakota way," I ask, "or *wasicu*?"
He blinks and turns away.

I am praying now
to any lord who listens
for lunch, for three o'clock
for poems, for patience.

Looking for Grandmother

I've wandered this dusty burying ground
for an hour, back and forth among the granite
stones, pink quartz, squares of shattered concrete,
but cannot find the plot of earth that bears her name.
And yet I greet her every day in my own kitchen.
I use the towels she folded on the shelf above the sink,
gifts from folks who cared for her but didn't know
what she would need or want. I'm wearing out the frayed
ones first, as she would do. Eighteen years after she died,
I still haven't had to buy a kitchen towel. Last week
I finished up her last jar of Noxzema, finally
old enough to be someone's grandma; old enough
not to care how I smell in bed. When all her towels
and bars of soap and lotion are gone, I'll still
be using her bread bowl, her potato peeler worn so thin
it's nearly wire. In my own looking glass, I see her hair,
the strong bones of her face. Her wedding ring gleams
on my cousin's left hand; she's younger. My knuckles
are swollen thick and growing thicker, more like
Grandmother's every day. Somewhere in that little town
below this hill, she once ran a dining room. Finally
there she is: just below the water tower.
The dusty stone reads Cora Belle.

Lost in the City Again

*The only time I ever read a weather report is when I'm outside
Montana, chanting my prayer: Dear God, don't let me die away
from my own latitude.*—McCarthy Coyle

I look away from the sign
to the art museum,
determined to meet
this final challenge.
If I follow the map,
look only at street signs,
I can escape this city.

Left on Hennepin feels wrong.
Clouds suffocate the sky.
I see no sun, no prairie light.
Clues collect until the signs say East.
Humming tires reverberate.
Horns blare, lights explode like sirens.
Gray buildings tilt my head back.
I look at the map, trace a way—
but the street's torn up,
I detour, detour again.

Once you're lost,
the problem in finding a way
is learning where you are.
These street names are
not on any map I have.

At a gas station,
I choose a man with friendly eyes.
Smile humbly, biting my tongue,
while he explains
why blondes are always lost,
before directing me.

Once I'm headed right,
I know by signs without words:
dairy barns turn into antique shops,
pastel houses cluster along gravel lanes.
By the time I'm passing warehouses
I see the landfill up ahead.
As far as I can see, the highway's flanked
by regiments of smoke stacks.
I hit the gas, keeping company
with eighteen-wheelers rumbling west
against the wind. Fields slope
in all directions. Trees forsake the road.
At last, the sky opens its arms.

Robbing the Poet

I met Sylvia soon after the burglary.
She'd come home after teaching all day
to find her house neat, but empty—
as if, she said, they'd taken time
to choose the best, or she'd hired movers.
They took her couch, chairs, bureaus.
As we walked through her rooms,
she waved at spaces, told me
what used to be there. Beds, sheets,
sets of dishes: Gone. Every room
was stripped, she said, except
the den where she writes poems.

Nothing was missing from that room—
she gestured toward the door,
but didn't open it. Throughout dinner
we considered thieves' choices.
"They left the art," she mused,
telling me every artist's name,
"and all the books." The door
stayed closed.
     After dinner,
we walked the river bank, talked
self-defense. I carry a pistol,
but Sylvia shook her head
at that idea. Over brandy,
we considered locks, read
each other's poems. For hours
we raided her shelves for books,
quoting lines to make our points.
The door stayed closed.

Finally, I unrolled my sleeping bag
on the carpet, over dents
left by the couch she used to have.

"That was a great couch," she said,
opening the study door. "Comfortable."
Laughing, she said she keeps a pad
and sleeping bag under her desk,
tucks a fire extinguisher close against
the wall. Then she closed the door,
shutting herself in
with everything the robbers scorned.

Leaving at dawn, I wrote a warning
on her door: "Beware!
In the dark behind that final door
is an angry woman,
finger on the foam trigger."

Snowed-in Psalm

No one can call me;
no one knows where I am.
I don't have to feed—
or love—anyone.
Outside, snow falls hard,
and a frozen foods truck
is still running,
but I have stopped.

Snow piles up on my pickup,
sealing me inside
covered walkways
to the souvenir shop and café.
Phone lines will go down.
Highways will be blocked.
I'm trapped—but
I have a ream of paper.

Writing poems,
I hyperventilate through my left nostril
because an article in a magazine
in the lobby said that's a sure way
to cure depression.
                              Just for a change,
I inhale through my right nostril.
Sure enough, I'm depressed.

I consider tiptoeing outside
in my nightgown to raise the hood
of that running truck,
jerk a wire loose.
Instead, I let that rumble rise
through the soles of my feet,
mutter into my veins,
flutter in my heart,
growl into every line I write.

Spider Woman: Canyon de Chelly

Spider woman sings the ages,
drones the sandstone turrets,
hymns the hogan in the canyon.
Croons wind, water, lizard claw,
horse's hoof, hand of man, wind.
Spider Woman stays.

Spring flood: a braided track
laces the canyon bottom,
quick water on the peach trees.
The potter gets her share,
kneads the clay, humming soft.
Light slants across
a fractured wall.
Night fills up the canyon.
Spider Woman waits.

Clay remembers hands
that sifted earth.
Clay recites the shape
of hands, of time,
of dust and water.
Spider Woman saw it all,
sees it now. Spider Woman
hums and weaves,
and
Spider Woman
waits.

The Story We Told Each Other in Zion

—for Jeanne

My old white bus
took us deep into a desert
where we'd never been,
our fingers cracking
like the mud in dry arroyos.
One day we heard a fall of water
splashing, a flimsy drapery
veiling a rough cliff face.
Forgetting scorpions,
we kicked off our sandals
and waded out to stand
beneath the trickle.

Our hands were pale
as the bellies of those frogs
that burrow into sand
and wait for years
for rain, for life.
Water soaked our skirts
and dribbled down our legs
until we laughed aloud.
The rare downpours of centuries
had chiseled cracks, carved doorways into wombs
where rivers might vanish into dusk.
Damp hair clung to our necks
like the fine ferns growing in the shade.

Our bodies, you said then, are only
fragile sketches of the earth.
Stone and bone are etched
by wind, baked dry beneath the sun.
Looking deep into the canyon's eye,

we felt the years ahead expire in sunlight.
Later, in a moonless night,
our turquoise rings seemed to shine
like the blue doors in the pueblo.

We told each other and our friends
we got home safe,
but our harmony was lost
along those broken highways.
Now when I think of you,
I forget the way days clashed
like cheap bracelets on a skinny wrist.
Peering west into an arid wind,
I squint and try to see the place
where we two tawny women,
hair flowing loose like horses' manes,
lean into a subtle drift of blue
and laugh the dust away.

Taos Pueblo, 1968

A man wrapped in a cotton blanket
met us on the road
took the entrance fee
and said a camera would cost extra.
Nearly broke, we locked
the camera in the car
already ashamed to be staring
at the way the pueblo people lived.
Some folks kept their cameras raised
before their faces,
in front of their eyes.
       We touched
a beehive oven, found it hot.
Startled by a screen door slam,
we faced a smiling woman,
scarf tied tight about her knotted hair.
She knelt before the oven, lifted out
ten crusty loaves. "Come inside,"
she said, and held the screen door open.
The muscles in her back flowed slow
as heavy oil. She gestured us to chairs
ready at a table scoured soft.
With strong brown hands
she broke one loaf,
set knives and butter down.

We ate while she arranged more loaves
on shelves against the wall to cool,
then came to stand beside me.
She touched the turquoise ring I'd found in pawn.
"Your ring looks like a little 'dobe house
surrounded by green hills," she said.
We smiled back at her, paid
what didn't seem enough.

Beside the church, a sign
informed us that the bullet holes
remained from the revolt
of 1847, ignoring half the tale:
the way the pueblo people
filled Charles Bent with arrows,
scalped him while he lived,
then burned the church
and all the whites inside.
Behind us, tourists
took pictures of each other
pointing to the bullet holes.

Driving off in silence,
we still could taste the bread.
We still could taste the blood.

Ravens' Knowledge

"Raven's knowledge:" in Irish lore, "to see and know all."

I.
Last night I dreamed
a million ravens flew
around my bed. Each one
cawed, "Just a minute.
This will only take a second."

Today I'm speeding south.
September lights the road
with ragged sunflowers,
yellow rabbitbrush,
glowing purple aster.
A raven drops
out of a cloud bank
just ahead, barrel rolls
and lands in a juniper.
Rain blasts my windshield.
The raven hunches,
fluffs his feathers,
leaps into the air
to fly beside me.
"If you're not busy," he remarks,
"Could you tell me how
to get my poems published?"
He lifts his wing; a fat manuscript
splatters on my windshield.
White pages lift like wings as I speed on.
I whip the car around a curve,
skid across the road, fighting the wheel.

When I look again, I see
only rolling clouds. One mile; two.

I keep checking my rearview mirror
until I'm sure I've lost him.
Beside a trash barrel, I stop the car
to walk the dog, myself, to stretch,
to feel the rain on my face.
Before I can turn the engine off,
or roll the window up,
a raven hops like a windup toy
across a picnic table,
bouncing as if his legs are springs.
I laugh. Madness, to think
the ravens are pursuing me.
"Raven," I say, "I'm sorry
I misjudged you. Give me
your wisdom. Can I escape
from the northern chill?"

"Let me tell you," the raven shrieks,
"about my conversion to the one true faith."
He leaps toward the window,
beak aimed at my eyes.
I jam the car in gear
spray mud and gravel fifty feet
leave rubber sizzling on the road.

At San Antonio Mountain, the clouds
begin to lift, sunlight slants
across the rock; the highway steams.
I sing a little, pass a truck.
In a hayfield, a crowd of ravens stand,
wings outspread, panting.
As I pass, the sun is darkened
by their black cloud rising.
"Kra!" they yawp together,
shattering the sky,
black wings beating thunder.
I duck and swerve
to miss a vampire pretending

it's a raven, hovering
above a cholla. Shadows
drop, covering the peak. Inside
the gloom, I know the ravens wait.

II
Today, my dog beside me,
notebook in my hand, I lean against
a ponderosa pine, split by lightning,
charred by fire. A raven lands
above me, tilts his head to rasp
a caustic cry. Another raven
answers from the canyon wall.
The gravelly river mutters
softly, whispers words
I do not understand.
Here, I am a stranger. Time
to scratch behind the dog's ears,
time enough to study
what the raven knows.

Making the Best of It

The big house we built together
encloses more space than a widow needs.
I left behind that roomy office
filled with gadgets guaranteed
to ease the writing life.

I erased my library,
deleted my kitchen,
omitted the waterbed,
abolished closets,
canceled my pantry.
I murdered my house plants
struck out comfortable chairs
dropped magazine subscriptions
voided the telephone,
annulled couches,
pillows, friends,
and locked the door
behind me.

In this village where
no one speaks my language
I live in a single room.
Inside my four walls
a straight-back chair faces the desk,
a lamp illuminates a rocker.
My skirts and t-shirts hang
on pegs in the adobe wall.
A chest with narrow drawers
accommodates underwear, socks.
Our dog is curled on my pillow
on the single bed
beside the window.

In this place, the hills above me
inhale air you never breathed,

exhale crisp breezes all day long.
Light strokes my face at dawn,
outlines the pages of my books,
skims the rocky peak.
In the field beside the house,
a man, a woman, and four children
pitch hay into a pickup truck.
In shade on the covered porch
I watch and write
compact words that seem
to form themselves in lines.
Paragraphs scale the walls.
On the tawny cliff before me,
I witness each day live and die,
and never calculate its whole.

Visiting the Nursing Home

—for Josephine

Water batters the roof.
Inside, echoes ring loud
as the cane tapping the corridor.
I hesitate, afraid of what I'll see,
what I might do.
I have no right to what I feel.

Before I'm ready, I see my Aunt Jo
at a table in a sunny room.
She tries to glue a scrap of lace
to an embroidery hoop—
a task contrived to challenge
damaged minds, tired fingers.

She was always too busy for crafts—
pulling calves, mowing hay,
baking harvest pies.
Even when she married well,
she kept her own checkbook and accounts,
marked cattle with her private brand.

Her long red fingernails
are tangled in the fraying cloth.
She always wore them short,
never owned nail polish.
Some kind aide worked
as hard to paint her nails
as she does now,
and to as little purpose.

An aide snatches her hand,
holds it down on the table
against her struggles,

clips her fingernails short.
I almost speak, but Josephine does not.
She would never let anyone do
what she could do herself,
but I have no rights here and
she is not the woman I once knew.

Seven other women
sit with her around the table,
ghosts of their experienced selves.
Weary voices rise and fall
in symphonies of patience.
The dead air stirs and sighs.
Six hundred years of wisdom
ebbs from brains and fingertips.
Nothing I can do
will replace what she has lost.
We who knew her
must remember what she can't

No one ever left her house
without hot coffee, chocolate cake,
butter-rich pie crust cradling apples.
She dug the trees from an old orchard,
planted them on the dry plain,
soaked the earth with dish water
when the well went dry.

One cold winter day,
I moved cattle with a neighbor
through a blizzard.
We warmed ourselves before her fireplace
eating rum-soaked fruitcake.
Laughing, we raced our horses
through the drifts,
joked the fruitcake made us tipsy.
We didn't know we'd filled ourselves
with all the love she had to give.

Instead of a Death Watch

—again, Josephine

I. What She Doesn't Say

My aunt, who hasn't spoken for several days.

> "It's all a mistake. If I'd only known.
> I always decided what would happen
> to me, to people I cared about."

Uneasy, relations lean against white walls.
Beneath their talk, I hear her whisper.

> "Harold would have died that time,
> if I hadn't yelled until they took him
> to a better hospital."

Her brain heaves with breeding tumors.
Tubes carry air into her body,
waste out. Nurses watch a screen
where colored lines sketch life that is not hers.

> "If I'd known, if I'd only known," she whispers.
> "I'd never have let it happen this way."

Today I've agreed to give a speech
halfway across the state. I'm packing
when my mother calls to say
the family is gathering at the hospital
—again. "You can't leave,"
my mother says. "What if she dies?"

What if she does? I said
goodbye while she could hear me.

Fleeing deathbed scenes
I drive too fast.

II. What She Says

> "Look, that fellow's got his hay stacks
> in a bunch by the house; one lightning strike
> could take all his winter feed."

Wait a minute, I say.
You're not supposed to be here.
You're supposed to be back there dying
where the family's gathered around your bed.

> "That next place is empty;" she says.
> "A shame. Folks worked hard, lost it anyway.
> Nice place for a house; look at the view."

I can't look; I'm driving.
Since I'm hearing voices,
maybe I shouldn't be.

> "Some woman worked hard to keep those flowers alive,
> just like I did. All winter, looking out the window
> at brown stems, I pretend the snow drifts
> are white blossoms in spring."

Her voice rises, falls like the tawny grass
beyond the windshield. I gather my nerve,
and glance at the seat beside me.
She's there, brown curls blown in the wind.
Grinning, tan face crinkling,
She throws her head back in a laugh.

> "Well, we fooled them, didn't we?
> They're all gathered around that bed again,
> trying not to look at that mess hanging under it."

That's where you're supposed to be, I tell her,
instead of making me talk to myself.

She shakes her head. "Nobody touches me
but the nurses. You'd think it was catching."

I'm not happy talking to the dead either,
I say. Leave. Shoo. Scram.
For once, she's quiet, looking at me.
Maybe she knows that two years later,
I'll welcome her voice
when I pull a calf at midnight,
and talk to my dead husband every day.

We meet a Cadillac;
a tumbleweed wide as the grille
rides the radiator,
twined into every crevice.

"Look—that's how that tumor is inside my head,"
she says. "For years, that thing's had its claws in me."

Your grandfather kept a journal, I tell her,
though she knew it once. When you were born,
he wrote about the tumor on your head.
Maybe it's been waiting all these years.

"It waited a long time, then," she cackles,
voice trailing away.

Sunset gilds the rolling slopes along the road;
shadows lie along the river.
Ahead, I see her striding up a hill,
sun burnishing the hair gone months ago.

"You be sure somebody waters those trees
I planted," she yells over one shoulder.
"And don't forget . . ."

She tops the hill, strides down
into bare white cottonwoods
along the wide Missouri,
rolling high with snowmelt,
thundering toward the Gulf.

Though I can't hear her voice,
the land and river
know where she's gone.
But just in case,
I say goodbye for her
to big bluestem and redtop,
buffalo grass and grama—
standing up to the west wind.
The engine rumbles as I top the slope,
still heading east.

My Uncle Harold Makes Up His Mind

The house they built
together booms with TV voices
loud enough to fill the rooms
where their children never played.
Before his wife died,
she said she felt like rats
were eating her brain.
He props his crutches
against the chair,
looks out the window
at thirty fat Hereford cows.
Since cancer took his leg,
he drives the pickup while
the hired man pitches off the hay.

The hired man has three kids,
lives in the little house
across the yard, next to the corrals.
He's buying the ranch.
My uncle tells me how he built
that old house for his mother.

Right then, he decides out loud
it's time to let the family move
into the big house. He nods.
"I'm going to move back," he says,
"back to where
I drove all the nails."

Valentine For My Mother

I.
Cut flowers don't last
says a woman's voice.
I spin around in the Safeway aisle
expecting to see my mother
who's been dead all winter.

Cut flowers don't last,
she says again,
the woman with blue hair
beside the flower display,
shaking her head at the young man
still reaching for a bouquet
wrapped in red paper.

She sounds like my mother,
mouth pursed, not smiling,
each time I brought a bouquet
to the nursing home. You shouldn't
have spent the money, she'd say.
Cut flowers don't last.

I picked them
from my garden, I'd say.
She'd snort.
Cut flowers don't last.
So I brought slips
from my plants,
potted them for
her window sill. She didn't
give them water.

II.
When I was growing up
Mother served our meals on Melmac

scrawled with scratches,
kept the good china
in the cupboard
so it would last.

During that final year
she was alive, she asked once
about her good china. Safe
in my glass-front hutch, I told her.

At ninety-two she took her final breath.
I covered her pink enamel coffin
with roses the color of every blouse
she gave me no matter how many times
I told her I hated pink.
As I paid the florist
with her money, I told him
Cut flowers don't last.

III.
Now in the Safeway aisle
I smile at the young man
who is carrying the flowers
toward the checkout stand.
Cut flowers don't last
she says once more.

Tomorrow all the blooms
that do not sell will pucker
in the dumpster
brown as the roses whipped
by the cemetery wind
the day after my mother's burial.
Cut flowers don't last
I muttered to the mound
above her heart.

IV.
I gave her dishes to my cousin's
daughter. In my gardens,
I cut flowers, thinking of my mother.
Blooms scent every room,
reflect themselves even
in the bathroom mirror.
Every night from the arbor
I watch the sunset
that will never come again.

Cleaning the Stove

Pouring coffee, I hear the news:
another shooting at another high school.
Instead of sitting down to listen
I fill a bowl with water that's too hot.
At the stove, I wet the rag,
force myself not to flinch,
begin to wipe up grease.

More than once in this Old West town
I've seen high school boys in dusters.
I've imagined how the coat swings
as he turns and fires, heard the screams,
could almost see the blood.
Wiping the stove top beside
simmering chicken soup, I hear
more details: he's killed ten people,
including his own grandfather,
a tribal cop. His father killed himself
years ago. Some commentator
mentions Prozac, already explaining
how this boy's story
was seared with trouble,
burning into darkness.

                  Until today,
it might have gone another way.
Faced one day with some angry,
frightened kid, he might
have paused, remembering.
                  Until today.

Grease floats in the sink. I run
more hot water, squirt more soap.
A thousand miles away, I hold my hand
in water hotter than I can bear
and clean
this stove.

Chin Hairs

Two o'clock each October afternoon,
the sun angles just right
through the bathroom window
so I can perch on the tub
with the magnifying mirror
in one hand and the tweezers
in the other to pluck
hairs off my chin.

Each day, when I look in the mirror,
I see my grandmother.
Of course we never talked
about our chin hairs.
During our final conversation,
she was too old, I too young,
our minds too busy with her dying.
But these days we each know
what the other is thinking.
We understand how fast
the sun is sinking into winter.

Sitting on the side of the tub,
I remember being blonde,
believing chin hairs to be the curse
of dark-haired women. I tweeze
and yank and pull
and mumble to myself.

After I pluck awhile, I return to my desk.
I don't know the angle of the sun
where grandmother is,
but I'm sure
no chin hairs grow.

Studying Pumice

Pumice is igneous rock blown
out of the throat of a volcano. Open
the new package of rubber gloves,
slip my hands inside. Super-heated,
highly pressurized, pumice explodes
upward, bubbling, hissing. Kneel
on the rug. Open the cardboard box
over the toilet so the pumice dust
falls inside. Pumice is the only stone
that floats on water. Watch it bob gently.
Rub it against the toilet rim. Rust
flakes away. Pumice fibers or threads
may lie in parallel rows, with intervening
threads to form a delicate structure. Scrub
around the top edge of the toilet, grinding
away rust, curving the pumice to fit
the smooth porcelain bowl. Pumice is
produced by the expansion of the internal
gasses of lava when they reach the surface
of the earth. Take your time, as lava takes
time to form. Remember the women who
have done this job forever, without gloves.
Flush. Close the intake valve before the bowl fills.
Change hands. The word *pumice* is derived from
the Latin word *pumex*, meaning foam.
Around and around the curve of the bowl
rub the pumice, rocking it over the undulations.
Pumice is lava froth, glass foamy with air,
cut and packaged for sale with instructions
in English and Spanish. Shift from one knee
to the other. Scrub. English and Spanish.
Open intake. Flush. Close intake. Breathe.
Scrub, reaching deep. Outside the bathroom window,
a meadowlark calls in sunshine. Fine
ground pumice is used in toothpastes
hand cleaners. My knees ache. I flush
grains of lava from the earth's blazing heart
away.

Those Thanksgiving Pie-Makers

All over America today, women search
for their grandmother's pumpkin pie recipe.
Some rush to the store for condensed milk,
or whipping cream. Or stir up powdered milk
if they are poor, or on a diet,
or live too far from town.

In a Wisconsin farm house a red-haired woman
measures salt in a dented spoon.
In California, a thin girl stirs and puffs a cigarette,
puffs and stirs. In Wyoming,
I dust clove powder over my grandmother's
green glass bowl and reach for the nutmeg grater.
In New Mexico, a brown-eyed woman
sprinkles cayenne. In Iowa, a man beats eggs,
recalling for his children how their mother looked.

Grandma always left me to measure
dry ingredients while she walked down
to her hen house. She came back holding four
warm brown eggs in her open hands
just as I licked brown sugar off my lips,
thinking she wouldn't notice.

So today, twenty-five years after she died,
I lap brown sugar from a spoon just
so I'll remember how she grinned at me.
While I stir, my oven beeps. Hers
was fired with wood she chopped. To test
the heat, she'd dip her fingers
in the water bucket she'd pumped full
that morning, flick spattering drops, and nod.

All over America, families are studying
gratitude. Some women slip

a pie into the oven, and hide
the cardboard box in the garbage.
Others light pumpkin-scented candles,
thankful anyway—though my grandmother
might not think they have good reason.

I crimp the rim of each pie crust
with three fingers, just the way
she taught me; make a salad
while the fragrance surges out
the open kitchen window. Next door,
perhaps the drug dealers open their eyes,
inhale, and almost remember.

Grandmother, may this pumpkin perfume
rise up to whatever heaven you inhabit,
sanctifying all my love and memories.
Listen: countless voices chant together
an infinity of thankful hymns.

Bacon, Lettuce and Tomato

First bacon, lettuce and tomato sandwich
of the season makes me think of you.
Walking to the garden, we'd argue
smiling, choose sun-struck tomatoes.
I'd wash the lettuce; you'd arrange
thick bacon strips in the black pan,
toast homemade wheat bread,
slather butter. I'd slice tomatoes,
smear Miracle Whip. You'd turn bacon.

You said you wanted Elvis to sing "My Way"
at your funeral. I promised to see to it.
What would you say about the election
coming up? Maybe you're saying it,
but not to me. Today I don't even know
if you're alive. I'm toasting cheddar bread
I bought at a market stall, slipping
nasturtium leaves among the lettuce,
but I still use Miracle Whip.
Have your sandwich your way,
wherever you may be.

1971: Across From the Packing Plant

Across the street, another truck
grinds its gears and backs up to the chute.
The doors of the packing plant bang back.
Four men climb the truck's sides,
swear and prod and club the steers
so each one bawls and struggles as they turn
and squeeze together through the gate,
scramble up the ramp to balk at darkness
inside the room they'll never leave.
The knocking of the hammer pounds
a cadence, howling death and blood.

I sip my tea and stare across the street.
The steers' hooves hammer
tempo to my rage and fury.
I have been six years a faithful wife,
have left my husband one more time
to hide on this back street,
this dim apartment upstairs
in an old house in Columbia, Missouri.
At first, I liked the smell of cattle.
The trucks, the rugged men in jeans
reminded me of home, the ranch I'd left to marry.
But now the trees are leafing out.
I know too much.
I sip my tea and think of sunset
behind the prairie swells of home,
light that surges up the sky the way
the morning meadowlark greets dawn.
I swore to love and honor but
this time I cannot take him back.

Tonight my husband will put on
a shirt of silk I bought him, dab
cologne behind his ears and go downtown.

In a dark piano bar
he'll croon love songs all night long,
take some girl home with him
and love her in the house we chose together.
Will he remember to walk our dog?
Will she scratch behind the dog's ears?

The steers have all gone through the door.
Now they stumble down the chute
to meet the knacker with the sledge
that slams against the forehead of each steer,
dead center. The steer's legs fold. Another
man loops chain around the steer's back legs,
secures the hook and yells. The lift man
pulls a handle, jerks the steer and swings
him upside down and hangs him on
the bloody killing floor. Each time a steer
flips upside down, he bawls, a moan
that startles me so much I spill my tea.
The long groan rises with the arm
that swings the steer and lowers him
and stops in gushing silence on the floor.
The last man cuts his throat, jumps back.
The cadence of the hammer pounds
a pulse of heated blood inside my brain.

At break time all the men come out
to lean against the wall in bloody aprons.
They roll distorted cigarettes
and smoke and spit and nod politely at me.
They tell me that the first blow knocks
the steers out cold, unconscious, so they don't
feel pain or struggle. Why then do
they bawl? I asked them once.
They shrugged and looked away.
All reflex action, one said.
The quick ascent propels the air
out of the lungs. That's all it is. They nod together.

The knocking of the hammer has begun
delivering its metered message.
Tonight my husband sings the songs
he used to sing to me, but I hear death
across the street. Another steer
begins to moan. I step outside the door.
Soon the butchers will come out to smoke.
They'll hang their gory aprons
by the door and wipe the fresh blood from their shoes.
And all night long I'll hear the hammer beat
its rhythm, and the howl of blood and death.

1971: Establishing Perpetual Care at the Locust Grove Baptist Cemetery

A knock at the front door
echoes in the landlady's empty hall
tinkles past the crystal in the cabinet,
drums across her kitchen floor to mine.
She's not home. Whoever it is will come
to my door next. I stretch,
drop the pen and fill the kettle.
Light the stove with a wooden match.

A stooped man in a black suit
rounds the corner, dust rising
behind his cane with every step.
Ancient sweat stains streak
the band of his straw hat
like layers in old sandstone.
He shuts the gate behind him.
Thumps the door four times
with a rugged fist.
Straightens his shoulders.

I snap the bolt open,
but stay behind the locked screen door.
"Good afternoon," I say.

He pinches his hat with
two gnarled fingers, lifts, and says,
"Good day, Ma'am. I'm Walter Mathis
from up at Locust Grove."
He hangs the cane on one arm,
mops his forehead with a red kerchief,
tucks it in a shirt pocket. "Does Mrs.
Notye Murray still live here?"

He's afraid she's dead.
"Yes," I say. Adding the "Sir"

is automatic, involuntary even.
"That's her door you knocked on."

"She's not home, then," he says,
nodding. Just what he thought.
He squints, leaning toward the screen.
"You her granddaughter?"

"No sir, just a tenant—I rent
this back apartment," I say.
Because it's cheap, I think; because
I've left my husband
and have no money and no credit.
"When she goes out in the afternoon,
she's always back by dark," I say.
"Unless it's her whist night. But that's Thursday."

He leans back on his heels,
rapping the cane against the concrete step.
Eyes the packing plant fence
like he's tempted to get the hammer
and a fistful of nails out of the tool box
I know is behind the pickup seat,
fix the blasted thing so it'll stand up straight.
"Well," he mutters. "Let me think."
He yanks the hat brim down.

I unlock the screen door, step outside
to say, "She might be home earlier.
I'm not real sure where she was going
but if she went for poke salat
and lambs quarters,
she might be home pretty soon."

"Cooks 'em up with bacon, I bet,"
he says, grinning. "Bet you never had
vittles like that, beings you are a northern lady."
He nods. Another thing he knew

without even thinking.
I nod right back at him. The cane
pounds once more on the step.
His mind's made up. "Well.
I gotta be gettin back to Locust Grove
so you tell Notye—you tell Miz Murray for me.
We gotta get goin on this perpetual care
for the cemetery up there. Us old-timers,
we figure maybe the next generation
won't be as interested in the folks there.
But her and me, we got close folks—
she's got her ma and pa and husband up there
and all my folks are together in that one spot."

I nod again. Now I remember who I am,
even if I don't know where.
I can see the cemetery in my home town,
where once I could imagine
my husband's tombstone with mine beside it,
infinitely announcing our devotion.

He shoves the hat to wipe
his forehead on his sleeve,
yanks the brim back down. Nods again.
"Well, I live right by the cemetery, don't ya know.
Me an' Howard Breedlove and Walt Kinsolving—
that's my son-in-law—we all got together
cause folks been wanting to give me money
so there'd be some kind of continual care.
And I figgered if I just took money
even if I put it in a bank,
pretty soon some bank examiners'd
want to know what I'm doin,
and pretty soon after that
the income tax people
would come a'sniffin around.

So we formed an association. I'm president.
Yep. Howard Breedlove's treasurer.

I come down here today to get papers
drawed up and signed. And I wanted to tell her
if she wants to send a check
to make it out right, to make it out to
The Locust Grove Baptist Cemetery Association.
I always mow the lawn, mowed it
seven times last year, charged forty dollars
an they paid me OK, but the year before
I mowed it ten times an there wasn't
enough money in the treasury to pay me
so I just give 'em the last one.
I lived there all my life and all my folks
are buried there. I usually got
some grandchildren to help me.
About your size."

Walter Mathis waves his cane,
redeems me as his grandchild.
I'm ready to follow him home
to Locus Grove, learn to cook
poke salat just the way he likes it.

"Here now, you tell Miz. Murray
I come by and to make the check out
Locust Grove Baptist Cemetery Association."
He tips his hat again. "Good day to you, ma'am."

The kettle's boiling. While Walter's 1953 Ford pickup
lumbers down the street, I pour my tea,
take the cup upstairs and lean to look
out the bedroom window, to watch
until Walter Mathis turns left
on the gravel road out of town,
headed back to Locust Grove.
I sip my tea and know it's time
I headed home
where people recognize me,
where the cemetery dust
is folks I knew.

The Westie's Nightly Game

—for Duggan

The mangled purple ball
bounces off the planks, smacks
the little white dog's nose.
He shakes his head,
dives behind the hollyhocks,
bites and brings it back,
his plumy tail waving.
I kick again. Thwack
and bite and back again.

His pink tongue dangles.
He's not building equity,
or obsessed with hair loss;
he hasn't noticed the drug dealers
moving in next door;
doesn't care how much
our taxes have gone up this year.
On the street in front of the house,
folks rev their engines, heading home.
Work day over, people honk, curse,
squeal their brakes. Every dog on the block
barks and barks. Kick, thump, slap.
The Westie grins and runs.

Home: Ending the Day

—for Jerry, and for 2722 Warren Avenue

Home. The younger dog noses
my ankle as I open the refrigerator door,
put hamburger on the counter to thaw,
mash garlic on the chopping board
with the broad blade of the sharpest knife
the one I found in the trunk of my father's car
after he died, probably his mother's
butchering knife;
                        peeling and chopping garlic
I count the onions in the basket
hanging on the cupboard end, flaky gold skins drying
in this August heat, tip olive oil
into the biggest cast iron frying pan,
slide the garlic in to sizzle gently
the aroma winds through the hall,
spirals up the stairs with me and the dog to the room
where my computer hums;
                        the dog lies down,
sighing, dozing while I ponder and mumble
then he follows me downstairs to sigh again,
folding onto the rug while I mince onions,
stir them in with the garlic and oil,
inhaling deeply while I find tomatoes
in the pantry, trip over the dog,
dump them into the pan with oregano
I gathered last October, dried in dish towels
clipped to the window frames, crumbled now
in my hand with basil, parsley, sprinkled
over the sauce, stirred in with cayenne
before I go to the dining room window
to look out at the herb garden, at cars
passing on the street;

I glance at the clock he made
of aged oak on my way upstairs,
followed by the dog; I write,
sniffing the simmering sauce
for a couple of hours until he comes
walking into the fragrance, smiling
as he pulls off his tie while the dogs
tumble and bark, following him upstairs
in a running tussle, wagging and wiggling
and snarling at each other while he changes
clothes and I turn the heat low, put on the lid
to hold the bubbling scents while
we walk the dogs around the lake,
telling each other how our days went and
the dogs sniff trees and chase squirrels,
pant and grin while we each get a beer;

in the yard he listens while I speculate
on flowers that will bloom soon,
when the tomatoes will ripen
then we sit in the arbor waiting for sunset,
for the hummingbird moth to materialize
at the evening primrose, proboscis uncoiling,
rummaging deep, deep into the yellow centers,
invisible wings fanning air while we wonder where he sleeps,
decide whether or not to water the tree
we planted three years ago;
at dark we go inside, eat pasta drizzled with thick sauce
sit in our identical chairs to watch TV, read,
until it's time for him to mount the stairs with the dogs
all three tumbling into bed to snore
while I snuggle deeper in the chair
to read a little longer while the city
lies down around me;
I go barefoot into the back yard,
unwind my toes in wet grass,
breathe Artemisia until my lungs expand
and my eyes begin to close, wander back inside

to climb the stairs in darkness,
my feet knowing each carpeted step
my fingers brushing pictures, pebbled wall,
until I find my way to bed, shift one dog,
slip in beside the sleeping man,
safe at home.

On This Day

—Duggan, 12/20/2006

He lies beside my desk,
his toughened paws chasing
death. Every gasp reminds me
cancer fills his solid little body.
An emailed newsletter informs
me that on this very day
Ira Gershwin was born to write
those songs we can't forget.
My toes begin to tap
as fast as the sleeping dog
can run, to "I Got Rhythm."
Next I learn that on this day in 1907
an explosion in a coal mine
killed three-hundred-sixty-two men and boys,
left a couple of hundred grieving widows
and mothers, and a thousand orphans.
"Someone to Watch over Me," sings my brain,
a few beats behind my reading.
The dog sleeps quietly now,
heat ruffling his hair.

And that's not all.
On this day in World War I,
a ship blew up in Nova Scotia.
On this day the explosion killed
two-thousand people, did worse damage
than any of the bombs
dropped on European cities
during that whole war.
"I want my arms about you," sings someone
in my head. Faces flicker through my mind,
all the people I have loved

who are dead on this day—
millions I have never known,
lovers, husbands, parents, children,
all dead and remembered or forgotten.
On this day someone's dog sighs
and sleeps, a cat licks someone's tears,
snuggles close. I remember how pink
his paws were when I met him,
how soft. Now I can see in those cracked paws
all the miles he's walked with me.
One ragged little dog.

I whisper in his long white ears.
Of green grass, crisp snow to roll in,
good dogs he hasn't met, people
who will love him for me
until I come. He sighs.
                       And then he goes.

Sister Soar

I.
For seventeen years I've watched the scene
repeat inside my head as I drove into dusk
on highways everywhere. The memory
repeats; the ending stays the same; the poem
has never said the words I mean to say.

Black hair swaying, lips moving, you edged
onto the two-lane blacktop from a side road
twisting through Wyoming sage, made me
swerve to miss you. Then you passed too fast,
hurtling over the bumps. "California plates," I snarled,
"headed for the rez." I hoped a cop would
stop you. Just then, sunset gold lit the top
of Split Rock, dust billowed. Your car lurched
and rolled. Navajo blankets whirled,
settling like ravens on dry grass.

Suddenly, cars were everywhere. Tourist
campers spilled people running. Someone
drove a mile to find a phone and call
the sheriff. We found you shattered
on asphalt, covered you with a white quilt,
flower-embroidered. We dragged
your blankets and belongings off the road
and realized the bloody bundle on the white line
was your child. We slid him onto a red and black
design of thunderclouds, dragged him
to the shoulder. He whimpered
until a white woman with blue shorts
tight on heavy thighs lay down,
cradled his bleeding head, talked to him.
Another bathed his face. I brushed
mosquitoes away, covered them both
in more blankets. He said his name was Nicky,

said his arm hurt. Greasy men from oil rigs
and hay fields gently probed his pale arms
and legs. "I got some duct tape in the truck,"
said one, "an' some two by fours." Grim women
persuaded him to leave them there.

"Are you sure she's dead?" I asked
the air. Someone nodded, but I took
your slim hand, laid a finger on your wrist.
Blood warm, fingernails buffed smooth.
I expected you to squeeze against
my grip. I drew the quilt down softly,
afraid to wake you, cause you pain,
brushed aside a haze of black hair to touch
the thick vein beneath your fragile jaw,
then covered you again. Your feet looked
so chilled I pulled the quilt down, but that
revealed your face; the boy might see.
I tugged it up again, leaving your small feet
naked in the grass, striped with blood
until I covered them in my own
red and white blanket.

An hour we waited in the dark, waving
traffic by, murmuring to each other.
Finally: red lights, a sheriff's car, an ambulance.
The deputy's smooth young face was blank;
he took names, told us to move along. The crew
lifted the boy. The woman in shorts refused
to leave him. "But Joyce," her husband said,
"What am I supposed to do?" She didn't answer.
The deputy handed me my blanket. When
I looked back, he stood alone, badge reflecting red,
eyes scared. The white quilt shimmered;
your feet seemed to be moving.

Pulling out, I scattered sage and tobacco
out the window. My prayers spun

into night dark as your hair:
Wherever you are speeding now,
sister, soar. We did all we could for you,
and for your son.

II.
Seventeen years. I still carry that blanket
in my car. Somewhere the boy has grown.
I say to him, she was beautiful,
your mother. She made a mistake.
She went singing
into sunset.

Finding Mother's Jewelry

These were her favorites, the things I thought
I'd wear, so I saved them from the boxes
I hauled to Pac Rat Palace. I loved this black
onyx ring, a helmeted man who stares
in profile. When I asked where it came from,
she'd snatch it, shake her head and look away.
Now it only fits my smallest finger. This silver bracelet?
She murmured "MAY-hee-co" and smiled.
She rubbed her thumb over the fire opal
in silver filigree and hummed a tune I didn't
know. Both bracelets are too tight. Here's
bright orange branch coral. Did he give it
to her on their Hawaiian honeymoon, that drunk
she married first? My father. Didn't they go
to Mexico? She loved this branch of pink rhinestones
on her blue coat. She asked me to bring these three
rhinestone rings to her in the nursing home,
took off her wedding set and wore these instead.
She wouldn't tell me where she got them. I made
a list to account for every piece: "Eastern Star
pin, given to Hermosa chapter." The charm bracelet
draws me as it did when I was five: cups,
a bell, spoons and ollas, a lariat, sombrero,
and a padlock. I try it on: too tight. Once again
my father's legacy of big wrist bones and fingers
deny to me the treasures that were hers. And here's
the gold tin box from the bottom of her dresser drawer,
marked "Lipton Orange Pekoe & Pekoe tea bags."
Nine years she's lain beneath the only stone she owns,
where her name is carved in granite. It's time to take
this hoard to Goodwill. I'll add to the donation
this ring my first husband gave me; I hear he married
his fifth wife not long ago. I'll keep the tea box.

Scrubbing Cupboards

All over America, women kneel
spraying goo on the cupboards,
watch it drip down the painted pine,
wipe it off. Some grab a gnawed toothbrush
from under the sink, scrub around the faucet handles,
wiping brown crud away
with a dish cloth they'll bleach later.

Some women think this work so boring
they hire another woman—
usually one with dark skin—
to do it for them.

The rhythm of their work
courses through the veins
of those brown women,
of those women, and the ones
who can't afford to hire someone else
to do their dirty work.
The rhythms of their work surges
through their muscles,
ripples in their flesh,
barrels through their bones.

The bass notes of the songs
they sing mark the rhythm
for their arms, scrubbing, brushing,
scouring. The beat goes deep,
rumbling in the turgid water
flowing down the drains,
rising through the open windows,
humming into clean blue air.
Above the city streets,
those tunes twine and blend and pulse,
songs becoming symphonies,
thumping into alleluias,
pounding into marches.

Visiting Writer in Rock Springs, Wyoming

Inside, sixth graders rub
their foreheads on their sleeves.
Wrestling with rhyme,
they're losing ground.

The classroom air is thick
as cottage cheese. Metaphors
dense with hail and lit by lightning
grumble overhead. Rhymes
bounce off the windows,
stingers moist with poison.

Meter chatters as the fan blades
whisper, "Out, outside, outdoors,
remote, outbound, departing."

"Bring your paper and a pencil,"
I bellow, pushing past the startled teacher.
Spread across the grass we watch
a girl slim as wheat
ride a spotted mare
across the parking lot.
Slick as a minnow, the horse
slips between the cars,
carrying the girl away,
her hair woven like the prairie grass,
by wind invisible to us.

News of an April Day

Smashing garlic cloves
with a knife blade, I'm
looking out the kitchen window.
The skins crackle like
fresh newspaper
as a squirrel calls a news conference
from the apple tree.
Harassment, he alleges,
repeating himself in his fury.

Sidebar: the alleged abusers,
two white dogs, lie
(one in sun, one in shade)
drooling in dreams.

In other news, a robin
announces his candidacy
for Ruler of the World.

Meanwhile, our correspondent
in the cottonwood reports
a hawk has been cruising
the neighborhood.
Photos to follow.

Big bold headlines
announce a pasta sauce
so tasty your mouth
will remember it
all night long.
Film at eleven.

My Mother's Cosmos

Each spring I've sown
my mother's cosmos upon this city lot.
The seed I pull today from these bent heads
I'll plant next year
on land where she lived out her life,
and where her carapace remains.

We didn't get along.

The universe she chose did not include
the choices that I made: the way
I dressed and did my hair, my politics,
my taste in men. Still, I hope
she'll know how carefully I keep
this seed, and know I understand
how it contains so many worlds.
I hope she'll hear the words
we couldn't say, accept the way
the stalks that hold the cosmos
will bend, sometimes, to wind.

Sunday Morning

We kneel together on the mulch
inside the garden fence
marigolds keep watch, gold heads nod.
My golden head is mostly gray,
but hers is gleaming.
Her scissors flash as fast
as mine.

I'm a little creaky in the joints;
she's awkward with the coming child.
Clipping basil stems we talk of frost
the harvest of our hands.
Later my man makes lunch with bread
she baked: bacon, lettuce and tomato, mine,
lettuce, tomato, cheese for her, and
butter for us both.

We talk of what we've read, politics,
some reference to our mothers.
While she was growing up in Winnemucca,
I was grownup in Hermosa,
but we both know Mormons pretty well.
I'm moving soon; she'll stay.
In my new home, I'll plant and harvest
basil; I gave her seeds.
She'll bake; I'll miss that sourdough bread.
On Sunday mornings, we'll both
tend our gardens,
attending Basil Church.

When a Poet Dies

nothing happens.

A lesser poet
breakfasting on coffee
and a cherry strudel
picks up a newspaper,
turns pages to pass time.
After breakfast she will sit down to write.

The dead poet still lives
in a library in the living poet's mind.
His soft, strong voice just fills the room,
his books stand firm on shelves
arranged around a fireplace.
In the living writer's mind,
the poet she admires sits easy,
reading in an armchair
beside a sleeping dog.
The living, lesser poet turns newspaper pages,
seeking inspiration for a poem half as good
as any in those books by the poet
she doesn't know is dead.

When a poet dies, the living poet scans the news:
a couple of small, hot countries,
apparently unable to feed their populations
or cure disease, have declared war on one another.
Young men strut and posture in the streets,
waving rifles, shouting clichéd curses.
Civilian deaths have been reported.
Photographs show mothers scrabbling
in rubble seeking the bodies of their children.

When a poet dies, the governor, stern and pin-striped,
is considering a veto of the proposed aid-to-education bill.

Someone's daughter, freshly wed, peers
beneath a veil of newsprint, clutching the bouquet
she'll toss over one shoulder as she's led away to bed.

When a poet dies, the living poet learns that
a woman with a mouth as curly as her hair
has created a New and Flavorful recipe for Healthy Tuna Casserole.

When a poet dies, the live poet, feeling lesser still,
is about to flip the page, turning to the comics
and the crossword, when her eye slides down
the left-hand column to a two-inch block
of newsprint: Poet Stafford Dead.
She scans the lines:
"William Stafford . . . age 79 . . . 51 books . . ."
A second paragraph suggests he was
working on a poem the night before he died.
There is no photo of the gentle eyes,
the mouth about to smile, the strand of hair
that always stuck straight out.
The story does not mention how he said
to nearly everyone, "I'm keeping you on my radar,"
and did. But the lesser poet hears his voice, sees
how he reaches into his left shirt pocket,
unfolds a sheet of paper and begins to read
as if the poem were a letter, just the chatter
one might scribble to a friend—
what the grandchild said,
praise for some new poet,
his sorrow for the deer he'd found
dying on the road.

When a poet dies, the lesser poet, living still,
will stand before a student crowd two weeks later,
tears in her eyes as she says she'd like to read
a poem in honor of the poet William Stafford, newly dead.
In the front row, a teacher famous for his wit and toughness

will say aloud, tears sliding down his cheeks,
"He's dead? He's dead? When did he die?"

When a poet dies, no one lowers a flag,
or beats a muffled drum to the cadence
of the poet's best-known elegy.
When a poet dies, no one leads a riderless horse
down the avenue, spurred boots turned backward.
No one shoots the poet's typewriter beside the open grave,
tells the bees, frames the family photographs in crape,
hangs a black wreath on the door. Somewhere,
a publisher may nod and think Collected Works.

When a poet dies, the TV station's newest anchor person
may pat her hair, drop her voice, and say,
"The poet William Stafford died today at the age of 79.
And now—stay tuned for Sports and Weather!"
When a poet dies, the lesser poet reads
the two-inch story twice, while in her
mental library books tumble from the shelves,
awakening the dog. Flames tremble
in the fireplace, smoke twines around the chair.
Living on, the lesser poet sits before her desk,
remembers his advice: "When poetry comes hard,
lower your standards and keep writing."

When a poet dies, someone throws a stone
to vanish in a river rushing
over rounded rocks and driftwood.
In an eddy under willows, a circle grows,
spreading outward. Water laps the shiny hooves
of a mule deer doe stepping off a shelf of ice.
The ripple breaks against her nose
as she begins to drink.

A Venue of Vultures

Seventeen vultures perched all night
in the dead tree beside the gas station.
This morning I see them circling,
circling over the city, a kettle
on the boil.
                  Shivering
in September's sunrise, I pick
orange tomatoes beaded with moisture
—not quite frost, but close.
Fingers tingling, I align them
on the shelf under the kitchen window.
The clock says it's time to go.

In a car the color of fog I head north,
breathing deep, remembering the fall day
my husband and I saw twenty-three vultures
settle in the cottonwood beside my parents' house.
We all joked about the omens. Now
he's buried near my folks, closer
on cemetery hill than they were in life.

Still alive myself, I snap
Patsy Cline into the tape deck, hum
with Emmy Lou and Nancy Griffith,
hammer on the steering wheel,
bruising my hands to feel the bass.
Those women sing me through
this autumn sunlight, spin me toward
the rolling winter clouds.
We sing because we can.
We sing because we live.

Near the ranch, another sagging roof
has fallen in; another subdivision's
windows and garages gape above

the buffalo grass they will displace.
Blackbirds slide between the clouds,
wings so close they seem to brush my hair.
The grass glints yellow, green, brown,
green, red, green, brown, gone.

Autumn does this to me every time.
So many of the ones I've loved have died
as summer faded: grandmother, mother
father, best friend, husband. Sometimes
I dream of children.
There a pronghorn buck runs younger males
away from his band of does.
Yesterday I savored the last
tart rose hip on the bush. And there—
I count fast: twenty-four buzzards
jostle on that roadkill deer.

Here comes another fall
when I'm not settled where I want to die,
where I will watch leaves drop, snow sift down,
rain and sunlight come
again and again and again,
until I know in every bone the day
the sparrows will come back.
I want to tuck myself into that hillside
where I've loved and lost
and loved some more,
and keep right on living. Make
the buzzards wait.

Hawk in My Hand

A hawk
hangs from the wind
over the road ditch.

Looking up
I feel my own heart
pulse in my chest
in time with the hawk's
heart-beat in my wrist.

The hawk,
balanced on air
knows the heartbeat
of the mole.
The mole's veins
pulse with blood
made of plants.

The hawk tastes
the mole's heartbeat,
stoops and kills and eats.
The plant's blood,
the mole's blood,
throbs in the hawk's heart.

The plant,
the mole,
the hawk,
and the wind
drum in my wrist.

I hold
a hawk in my hand.

The hawk
holds me.

Signs of Civilization

I strap weights around my sixty-six-
year-old wrist bones, lift the back pack full
of dog leashes, treats, scissors, pliers and gloves.
The Westies run down the road ahead of me,
snuffling rabbit scent and gobbling scat. Cows across
the fence stare and chew. A garbage truck
pulls out of the subdivision across the highway.
I must remember to take the recycling
next time I go to town. Dew shimmers
on the grass. I walk around a spider's line
strung between two trees. The dogs
gather foxtail seeds in their feet and flanks.
I find a white feather with one stripe of black.
The dogs dive under the lilac bushes. Drumming
announces a car has hit the highway rumble strips
as the driver texts somebody from his cell phone.
Ahead I hear the clashing music, some kid screech
that he wants yuh, wants yuh, wants yuh. At the edge
of the garden, I turn off the radio, find deer tracks
but no damage in the corn. I unfold my knife,
cut new growth from the tomatoes, remember
how an uncle I barely knew taught me
this trick to make tomatoes ripen faster.
A monarch butterfly, wing torn, rests beside
the dill. Grasshoppers click on corn leaves. A mosquito
feeds on my ear. I'm the perfect age
to die from West Nile Virus so I smash it,
call the dogs and head back up the hill.
I hold my weighted arms out straight
and make slow circles as a cattle truck
grinds up the highway hill. A motorcycle burps
and passes. Back at the house, I pull
ripe gold cherry tomatoes from plants.
under the deck. A car leaves the subdivision
perched on gravel hills across the road,
headed to a job in town, won't be back
till after dark. I brush the dogs, pick two daisies,
and go inside to start a poem.

The Relatives Who Live in My Head

show up just as I slide into memories
of grandmother's smile as she basted the turkey.
They crowd into the kitchen
without invitation. They say
it's just not Thanksgiving without
Milly's broccoli and cheese casserole.
The truth is, none of them ate any of it.
Milly, my mother, elaborately ate one spoonful
that day, and we ate the rest for a week.

The relatives who live in my head say
it's just not Thanksgiving without
Hazel's oyster dressing. We all took that,
you bet, because Hazel would say,
"You missed the oyster dressing,"
and slap it on our plates herself.

The relatives who live in my head
are just like real relatives.
I don't see them for months.
They don't call, or write, or visit.
But come Thanksgiving, Christmas,
or Easter, here they are again.

The relatives who live in my head murmur,
"Only one kind of cranberry sauce?"
"Where are the green beans with slivered almonds?"
And what was that stuff on them—
cream of chicken soup?
                              "Sorry," I say,
but I'm not. They're muttering,
"No home-baked rolls? No sweet potatoes
with marshmallows and brown sugar?"

                    The relatives who live
in my head mumble, "That pie crust
doesn't look home-made." I hum as I
make a pasta salad. "What's that stuff?"
say the relatives who live in my head.
"Where's the Jell-o and marshmallows?"

"I love you all," I tell them,
"But buzz off," pouring
a wee dram of Scotch to sip
as I baste the turkey. My life mate
mashes the potatoes to creamy paste
swimming in butter. We seat ourselves,
brimming with thankfulness.

Autochthonous

Sego lilies still grow above the cedars
hidden in the gully. An old man in a rock shop
sells crystals just across the road from the pasture
where the jet trainer crashed forty years ago;
two pilots burned, screaming. Sweet peas
still bloom in Black Gap. Every spring
we picked some for my mother. When
the land was divided and house walls
began to rise, I said goodbye. But that black shale
won't hold foundations or septic tanks.
The houses slip and shift; their owners learn
more about construction and sewage every day.
I may see those blooms each spring as long
as I live. A thunderstorm leaps the hills,
gallops toward me. I dance in rain
under clouds headed for the Badlands
one more time. The grass that feeds those cows
on the hill twines through my flesh; the water
tastes of limestone percolated through
my bones. This sun leathered my face;
this wind wove the wrinkles at the corners
of my eyes. Each day the wind caresses me,
erodes a little more.

Ice Skating on the Dam

On a day like this, the sky flat gray
with hanging snow, we'd feed the cows
in pastures close to the ranch. Then
my dad would say, "Get your skates."
While he drove over the ridge, I'd take off
my work boots, squeeze my feet into stiff
white leather. Fingers freezing, I'd pull laces
while he shifted down for the steep hill.
He'd walk out on the dark ice and stamp
while I wobbled, clattered and screeched
across the rocks to the ice. He'd nod
and drive away, looking for the cows. I'd skate
up the draw until the ice was more grass
than water, race myself to the other end.
Arms out, I'd spin, sketch figure eights, stop short
so my jagged toes sprayed ice chips. "Shush"
said the wind or the blades as I spun
and slid, made gawky pirouettes.
The pickup horn honked closer as the dry cows
and old bulls bawled, gathering. Did he stop
to watch me skate? I'll never know.
He'd circle, scattering feed, as the cattle shoved
and grumbled, gobbling. Then he'd shoulder
the double-bitted axe, chop the drinking hole
until clear water bubbled up. We'd go home.
He's been dead sixteen years but I still
see him walk through the corrals,
shaking his head at missing posts.
After years of drought, the dam is full
this winter, deep water
frozen smooth and clear,
a great blue eye
that misses nothing.

Primer

Painting my new cold frame, I think
of Bill, who died this week. He lived
large every minute, prided himself
on drinking longer, singing louder,
playing the piano better. My knees crackle,
as I change positions. My knees
are the same age as Bill's knees.

Outside the window, geese talk
to each other, headed north in blue sky.
Twenty-three antelope, heads down, find
new green shoots. The twenty-fourth
watches me. Thinking of the lettuce I'll plant
in this cold frame, I realize that tomorrow
the pain in my knees will remind me
I am alive. A box elder bug like the one
he wrote an entire book about crawls
across my foot, red chevron matching the spatters
on my hands. "Hey, Bill," I say, "If you'd
taken better care of yourself, I'd write you
a postcard about this day and this fine bug."
I put the bug in sunshine on the window sill.

Girls at Fourteen

—for KD

I find it so much easier to say
what they are not:
they fuss their hair and smile
at their reflections in the glass
the way they think that women do,
but need a recipe to boil spaghetti.
Stir the pot and chatter just like wives,
but leave the stove all splashed in red
as if they'd fought a kitchen war.
They eat with grace and talk with charm,
so caught up in the topic they go off
to fix their hair some more,
leaving the dishes to congeal
upon the table. The older women
in the room smile at each other.

We women grown have learned
that if we want a footpath through the house
we'd better pick things up ourselves,
no matter who was there and made the clutter.
Mates and mothers automatically
straighten, tidy, wipe and dust. Some gripe,
while others do it silently. Just one
among the things we learn
that dim our smiles and bow our backs.
Not so these bright-eyed girls.
For them the lights still blaze in every room—
so many rooms they haven't entered yet.

We work together, clear the table
knowing soon enough the girls will learn
their lives require these mindless tasks.

For now, we let them go,
half-hearing their rhapsodic gossip.
They don't hear our giggles
as we wash and dry the dishes,
cheerful as we recollect the way we were,
before we thought of dimming lights and wrinkled skin.
If we can teach these girls that little things
don't matter, maybe they will laugh like this
when their young daughters are fourteen.
No need to nag at petty tasks undone.
They'll still be there tomorrow
and the days to come.

Wicca

Gray forms spring
over the flames' reach.
Red sparks flicker out.
Beneath the obsidian sky
we touch, pirouette, remember,
and give thanks.
Sage and sweetgrass smoke
drifts among pines
grown thicker than blood.
In the scrying bowl,
a single talon
pierces the moon,
scaly hide breaks the water's sheen.
Some of us will remember
our warm flesh tomorrow;
some of us
will still be cold.

Lost and Found

I started packing a year
before we moved:
this *here*, that *there*.
This box to the Salvation Army,
that box of family history
I'll want *someday* to the basement,
precisely labeled.

When I unpacked,
tools slid smoothly into places
I'd assigned months before;
clothes folded themselves on shelves,
drawers closed tight. My grandmother's
sewing basket settled itself on a table
by the window. But her tiny scissors
were not inside it.

Every six months or so,
I wake at sunrise,
sure that *this* time I've thought
where they must be.
I ransack boxes,
search a briefcase,
turn out another drawer.

This morning I dreamed them in her hand
clipping stitches in some blue-sky parlor;
see the black blades, that slim point
that fit into a single stitch, her age spots,
tendons. I'll never find them now.

All day I think of other things I've lost,
touch everything I love.
Before I sleep I say goodbye
to everything,
in case it's gone
before I wake.

How to Pick Green Beans

This morning's gold breeze slides
among beans slender as sunlight,
making snake patterns in the earth.
I brush leaves aside, careful
not to knock off blooms
that will make next week's beans.

Kneel
in the garden's deep soil.
Reach
to lift the bottom leaves.
Watch
for rattlesnakes.

Picking what she called a mess of beans,
my grandmother kept her hoe handy,
tilted her bifocals to see the snake,
steadied herself and chopped
until the hissing ceased.
Hooked him with her hoe, swung her arm.
The snake whirled and struck the sky.

Hold
each stem with the left hand.
Pluck
each pair of beans with the right.
One hand
should always know
the other's whereabouts in rattler country.

Redwing blackbirds sing from the cottonwoods
as I shuffle on my knees down the row.
Later, in the sinkful of water,
the beans sway like green snakes.
Grandmother used even the scabby ones,

hopper-gnawed. All winter, eating beans with bacon,
I will taste the green flesh,
taste the snake
within the harvest.

Reading the Newspaper

Two Marines die in mortar fire in Baghdad.
Four red tulips open in front of the house.
Searchers find the child dead—a green
plaster cast still cradles her broken arm.
Iris spears rise sharp above last year's
dry curls. An earthquake shakes L.A.
Clematis shoots from sawdust
to climb the arbor's trellised wall.
A soldier dies in a non-hostile incident.
Daffodils open beside the old cottonwood.
In Veracruz a gas leak kills six people.
Buds swell the twisted branches of a lilac.
A rebel bomb explodes in a crowd.
A Texas county's first female sheriff
is also Hispanic, a lesbian, and a Democrat.

Blue bells bloom
on the same day
as last year.

Priests of the Prairie

Whispering practical prayers for the dead,
the brotherhood meets in choir.
Girdled in righteousness, bony backs straight,
circling the funeral pyre.

Their dusty black tunics hang flat on their bones,
shoulder to shoulder they stand.
Tonsured heads wobble on scraggly necks
as they pray in the pastureland.

From out of the West, the priesthood has come,
cloaks shining black in the sun,
to gather around this altar of flesh
until their communion is done.

Their eyes see forever—and somewhat beyond;
eternity, and a square meal.
The Brothers of Buzzard are worshipping lunch,
devouring the finest of veal.

Morning News on Windbreak Road

We miss the rabbit who leapt up
beside the cattle guard each morning;
we found him dead yesterday.
The flax is blooming still,
corn is tasseling, peas are filling;
the mosquitoes vanish
as the grasshoppers multiply.
The raspberry bushes are
getting taller, but hoppers have
turned the rhubarb leaves to lace.
One Westie licks a frog;
he will spit all morning
trying to get the taste out of his mouth.
The orange tractor traces
the outline of the fence
as my man mows
a month's growth of grass.
Tuna salad for lunch, I think,
onions simmered in olive oil
to gentle them for our stomachs.
Peach ice cream tonight.
The cows are spread along
the ridgetop, dozing, grazing,
fattening their calves. Beneath
them runs the trail
the settlers' wagons followed
from Badlands soddies to the
stagecoach road. Great piles of rock
mark the edge, removed by men
to help the oxen walk in comfort.
We will never find
the pocket knife that slipped
as one man bent to place a rock.
A rattlesnake coils among cold stones,
full of mice, waits for evening
when he will hunt again.

Waiting for the Storm

Middle of July. Ninety degrees. No breeze.
Perfect haying weather said my father as we
leaned on the pickup passing a jug
of water back and forth. The burlap cover
I'd soaked at sunrise was dry, the water warm.
Fifty feet above us, green and yellow leaves
rustled in the sun, flung cottonwood shadows.
We stared westward, toward the Black Hills
trying to foretell the weather.
He told me how his dad came west in ninety-nine
with all those other Swedes and Germans,
settled in near Battle Creek,
began to learn how this Dakota country
differed from the flat black lands
they'd left in Iowa, where they'd paid
their immigration fare by working for their cousins.

With teams and slips they carved out
shallow trenches snaking toward the creek bank
from their fields; cautiously, they shaped them
so that only when a storm
dumped rain the channel couldn't carry
did the irrigation work. Instead
of roaring through the fences,
ripping off the sod, floods dribbled
into spreader ditches, soaking through their fields,
waiting for tomorrow's seeds. For years,
until the Dirty Thirties,
the rains that flooded Battle Creek,
spilled gently into ditch and field.
The settlers prospered, learned American,
saved their money, married local women,
and voted every chance they got.

The prairie wind spread every seed it caught;
Saplings sprouted everywhere along the stream.

Each trunk grew straight those first good years,
up twenty feet or so. Then, shouldered by prevailing winds
and stunted by the drought, they all began to bend,
to lean into a gentle curve. Wind conspired
with hail and snow and time against them.
Each tree now genuflects from north to south,
a row of arcs as even as the outline of a bridge.
"They look like little old ladies going to town,"
my father said, grinning. "All stooping in a row."
We watched a cloud bank rise beyond the Hills,
growing blacker as it towered toward the sun.
The old trees bent their backs, tattered women
hustling toward shelter, tipping toward the earth.
We laughed together; he was forty-six and I was twelve.

Blackbirds shrieked and billowed from the field,
clattering toward the streamside willows.
The air went still. Before the cloud
had covered half the sky, we felt a puff
out of the south, the land inhaling, summoning
the storm. We climbed inside the truck
and headed home. As I strained to close the gate,
rain splattered on my shoulders. The new hay lay
in windrows that would shed the water. When the field dried out,
we'd be back to finish what we'd started. Maybe we'd find
water in the spreader ditches.
                              Let's see now, that's been
forty-five years last July. Some of these old trees
must be a hundred. Their stooping line still charts
the ditch route, but I seldom see it flow. Too many
houses lie upstream, sewer lines draining into the creek.

One or two dead cottonwoods have fallen;
the rest are shaky, showing whitened trunks.
My neighbor, granddaughter of a frugal pioneer,
cuts the dead for firewood—but irrigates her garden
from the creek, water pumped with no permit.
I pat the nearest tree, feel how the bark is ridged,

wrinkled by her years, corrugated by her age.
Just like my skin.
                              My dad was pretty bent himself
before he died; my mother's curled into a comma.
Wheeling down the halls, she holds herself above the earth
as best she can, but not for long.
                              I straighten up
and pat the tree's old puckered hide once more.
A cloud is rising grim above the hills, a storm
that some of us won't weather through.

About the Authors

Twyla M. Hansen

Twyla M. Hansen is author of five books of poetry, including *Potato Soup*, winner of the 2004 Nebraska Center for the Book poetry award. Her latest collection is *Prairie Suite: A Celebration* from Spring Creek Prairie Audubon Center. Twyla is a creative writing presenter through the Nebraska Humanities Council and has conducted workshops, taught in residencies, and given readings to a wide variety of audiences in several states.

Her writing has appeared in publications such as *Cimarron Review, Crab Orchard Review, Flint Hills Review, Kansas Quarterly, The Laurel Review, Midwest Quarterly, Nebraska Life, North Dakota Quarterly, Organization & Environment, Prairie Schooner,* and *South Dakota Review* and included in *Nebraska Presence: An Anthology of Poetry, Encyclopedia of the Great Plains, Poets Against the War, Crazy Woman Creek, Inheriting the Land: Contemporary Voices from the Midwest,* and *A Contemporary Reader for Creative Writing,* among others.

Twyla grew up in northeast Nebraska on land that her grandparents farmed as immigrants from Denmark in the late 1800s. She received a MAg in agroecology from the University of Nebraska-Lincoln and lives, works, and writes in Lincoln, where her wild acre received the Mayor's Landscape Conservation Award. More information can be found at Nebraska Center for Writers web site.

Linda M. Hasselstrom

Linda M. Hasselstrom is the author of five books of poetry, including *Bitter Creek Junction*, which received the 2001 Wrangler in poetry from the National Cowboy and Western Heritage Museum in Oklahoma City. In 1989 she received the Governor's Award in the Arts and was Author of the Year for the South Dakota Hall of Fame. She conducts writing retreats at Windbreak House on her South Dakota ranch and was visiting faculty for the Iowa State University MFA in Creative Writing and the Environment from 2008–2011.

Her thirteen published books include *No Place Like Home, Between Grass and Sky, Feels Like Far, Going Over East, Windbreak, Land Circle, Bitter Creek Junction, Dakota Bones,* and *Caught By One Wing.* Her poetry and nonfiction have appeared in more than 100 magazines and in collections including *The Midwest Quarterly; Heart Shots: Women Write About Hunting; A Road of Her Own; Mother Earth: Through the Eyes of Women Photographers and Writers; Ranching West of the 100th Meridian;* and *Living in the Runaway West.* Information about her writing appears in *American Nature Writers, Dictionary of Midwestern Literature,* and *Such News of the Land: U.S. Women Nature Writers.* Her website, www.windbreakhouse.com, provides additional information.

CPSIA information can be obtained at www.ICGtesting.com
Printed in the USA
LVOW080417280113

317441LV00001B/5/P